FRIDAY BRIDGE

BECOMING A MUSLIM, BECOMING EVERYONE'S
BUSINESS

DAWN BATES

DAWN PUBLISHING

© 2017 Dawn Bates

Published by Dawn Publishing
www.dawnbates.com
The moral right of the author has been asserted.

For quantity sales or media enquiries, please contact the publisher at the website address above.

Cataloguing-in-Publication entry is available from the British Library.

ISBN: 978-0-9957322-2-3 (paperback)
978-0-9957322-3-0 (ebook)

Titles in The Trilogy of Life Itself:
Friday Bridge – Becoming a Muslim, Becoming Everyone's Business (2nd Edition, 2017)
Walaahi – A firsthand account of living through the Egyptian Uprising and why I walked away from Islaam (2017)
Crossing The Line – A Journey of Purpose and Self Belief (2018)

Book cover design – Jerry Lampson
Publishing Consultant – Linda Diggle

Disclaimer: The material in this publication is of the nature of general comment only and does not represent professional advice. It is not intended to provide specific guidance for particular circumstances and should not be relied on as the basis for any decision to take action or not to take action on any matters which it covers.

CONTENTS

For my dearest friend Amera, I love you habibti.
May you rest in peace… at least until I get there ;)

FOREWORD

For many people, September 11th 2001 is significant for all the wrong reasons because of the attack on the World Trade Centre. For me, however, this date is significant for all the right reasons as it was the day I first met Dawn Bates.

Young, confident and full of energy were my first impressions and whilst time does not stand still, the confidence and energy still remain undiminished nine years down the road.

I had the pleasure and honour to work with Dawn for many years during which time our relationship moved from being colleagues to one where I was able to guide her and help her begin to achieve her full potential. I say this in all humility because I know I learned as much from her as she did from me. I hope she's sitting down when she reads this as it's the first time I've ever admitted this to her!

'Fiery' is probably a good way to describe our relationship – but nearly always in a positive and constructive sense. Of course, with someone as driven as Dawn is, there are always moments when emotions get the better of rational thinking, but we always found a way to clear the air and move forward.

What I have always admired about Dawn is her determination and clarity of thought. Motherhood hasn't gotten in the way of what she wants to achieve in her life. In fact, I think it has spurred her on to achieve more – not only for herself but, more importantly, for her family. She probably wouldn't share this herself, but family is very important to her – be it blood ties or friends and colleagues – and this shapes the way she treats people (as well as the way she likes to be treated).

Dawn is one of those people for whom their moral code is highly developed and as such it influences everything that she says or does. From the heart or from the hip, Dawn has the potential to make a big difference in the lives of anyone she comes into contact with. Her journey to date has been full of highs and lows but Dawn has been able to take something of importance from every step of the way and reflect it back on those around her for all to benefit.

In conclusion, someone rather famous and clever once wrote about spending 'a day, a week, a month, a year' with people being important. Even just five minutes with Dawn is enough to have an impact on anyone's life – just remember to wear your seatbelt!

God speed, God bless – and I hope you gain something from her journey.

Charles Lovibond, November 2010

PREFACE

I feel an element of guilt about writing this book. Don't get me wrong, I've always had a love of books. I read on average four books a month. That doesn't include the, at least thirty, books I read with my children! Books for me are, some would say, not least my hubby, verging on an addiction. Put me in a bookshop and give me an endless pot of *proper* coffee, not the instant muck, and I will happily lose myself.

However, me being a Muslim is something my family would rather forget about, and at least one of them does not even want to acknowledge this part of me, therefore not acknowledging and accepting me as I am. Things they would rather just disappear from memory are written in this book, and unfortunately for them, books stay around forever. Add in talking about the 'disgrace' of my drug taking days, something which is bound to also offend my husband's conservative Arab family, and I'm sure you can see this book will cause us problems.

Even the fact I am writing a book, instead of just reading one, will also annoy my family, "Oh here she goes again, thinking she is so much better than us!" Well, if they truly knew me, they would know that I do not think I am better than anyone. I don't read books for the reasons they think, I read books because they can teach you a great many things, and they help you to escape into another world. I am comforted knowing the first word revealed to the Prophet Mohammad was 'Read', and read I do.

There have been many questions asked about why I converted to Islaam, considerably more than about why I took drugs even, which in itself tells you something! Anyway, some would say I reverted, me, I don't really care which word is used to be honest, I just know I chose a religion that had the one God, the Creator and it feels right. I am encouraged, through the unaltered words of the Qur'aan to question God's word and not to fear questioning. Although with many Muslims today you would think this not to be the case, but more on this later.

Many people think I became Muslim 'because' of someone else, mainly my husband. Many think I have 'become' Pakistani or Arab. Neither is correct. This book tells you why I became a Muslim. It tells you why the religion so many love to hate these days, is the one I chose to follow, and love.

It also talks about my dealings with drugs, depression, epilepsy, business, and motherhood. All within the framework of what it's like living your life as a White English Muslim Woman, or a Muslim White English Woman, or a Woman who just happens to be a White English Muslim, because I'm a woman whose faith has become the only identity she has. This may confuse you, believe me it has confused me. But I can assure you I am simply me. I am Dawn.

I have wondered many times whether I should actually write this book. I have wondered whether my journey is important or interesting enough to tell. The deciding factors have been the continued interest and questions from the media, and from the many people of all faiths, nationalities, cultures and communities that I come into contact with. The responses to the articles I write and talks I give have been positive and many have said, "You should write a book!" Well here it is, answering the intrigue people have as to why 'someone like' me would become a Muslim. I am not someone who is writing a book to show how good or bad I have been, just someone who simply wants to answer so many of the same bloody questions in one go, instead of answering them over and over and over again. If the business world has taught me something, it is to work smarter not harder.

My intention is to change negative perceptions of Islaam, and

Muslims, but mainly of Islaam. Islaam is not an evil religion; it is a peaceful religion that shows us a way to live our lives as individuals as well as communities. Islaam cannot be blamed for the way in which many Muslims choose to live their lives, just like the game of football cannot be blamed for the hooliganism and racism that infected it. Religion doesn't cause the wars; man does with his greed and ego. Religion doesn't have an ego and it cannot be greedy.

Now, while you read this book please remember: I am *not* an Islaamic scholar. I am simply a person who knew enough about Islaam to know I wanted to follow it as my guide through life. I am a seeker of the truth and if I find out along the way that Islaam is not the truth, I will take the good things from it and move on. I do my best, but I know I make mistakes every single day of my life, small ones and big ones.

If you listen to many of the sheiks, scholars and imaams around the world – oh, and of course all those 'well meaning' brothers and sisters who know 'every' Hadeeth and Sunnah (sayings and traditions of the Prophet Mohammad) – then remember, they all have their own take on Islaam, and they're entitled to it. It comes from their culture, education and understanding of history as well as of the Arabic language. But to be honest with you, I believe none of us truly know if we are right. I just have faith in my understanding of the unaltered word of the Qur'aan; God's word, not a monarch's, or man's, just God's. Pure and simple.

Traditional Muslims reading the last paragraph will have noticed I didn't put PBUH after the Prophet Mohammad's name. The PBUH, for those not in the know, is an abbreviation for Peace Be Upon Him. Now, as this is my book and I wish peace to be upon everyone (well most people anyway – Adolf Hitler and Ariel Sharon and those like them can go to hell in my humble opinion, but hey I am not God so who am I to say who goes where?), I will not use PBUH after the names of the Prophets. I will also use the word God rather than Allaah, as this book is written in English not Arabic and I see no reason to use an Arabic word when a perfectly good English equivalent exists.

There may, no, there *will* be things in here that offend people,

Muslims and non-Muslims alike, but hey, I wouldn't be a free thinker if I didn't offend people.

What is it Napoleon said? "A leader never stood for anything if he wasn't controversial." Well I know I am a leader. I know I am confrontational. I have a feeling many of the people I know will already be laughing as they read this part. Well good, I have brought a smile to someone's face already!

This book is written as naturally as possible. I use humour, analogies and the odd bit of sarcasm. I know sarcasm is the lowest form of wit, but it's okay, if you have no sense of humour you won't notice the wit anyway! As this book is for an international audience, I have added as footnotes explanations of terms or language that will probably mean nothing to someone from outside the UK. Even people from the UK will find terms from the subcultures they do not know about unfamiliar to them, so the footnotes should help them too. I am bound to have missed a term here or there, you'll just have to search the internet for their meanings!

This book contains *my* truth, the way I have felt and my opinions. This truth may be different from the truth of those mentioned in the book, but as we all know, or should know, truth is subjective and relative. Take a road accident for instance, four people see the accident from four different angles. The truth they see is relative to the position they were in, their personality, their mood, the time of day and many other variables.

I hope you enjoy reading this book as well as learn something from it. The books I love the most, are the ones that challenge me and leave me thinking about them, whilst also bringing a smile to my face. I trust this book challenges you and brings a smile to your face. In Islaam, smiling is seen as charity you receive blessings for, so to get you started here's a cheesy rhyme I've always liked:

"Smiling is contagious, you catch it like the flu, someone smiled at me today and I started smiling too."

I hope you enjoy the journey through the next 'few' pages, share it if you do, because if it speaks to you on some level, it will work for others too...

ONE

MY FIRST TIME

My Father was with me when I did it the first time. I was so nervous. I had never been so nervous about anything. Losing my virginity, taking drugs, getting married, giving birth, and speaking in front of 2,000 people following the international hip hop group Outlandish at a fundraiser, were all walks in the park compared to this moment.

I remember the stress, sweaty palms, stabbing myself in the head with the pins, scarf getting retied many times, and so much sweat I thought I could feel on my face, which wasn't there. My throat was really tight and I felt as though I was going to choke. I went to the toilet for an imaginary wee several times before leaving the hotel room. Finally I decided to just get a grip on myself and walk out the door. If the scarf needed retying again, fine, it could be done. I didn't need a wee, it was just nerves. From this day on, I would always wear the scarf, just get over it. So, I did. I walked out into the hotel corridor, got in the lift and hit 'G'.

I needed to eat even though I felt sick to my stomach. On the way down to breakfast, the lift stopped, a woman got in and in my nervous state I started to leave, realising I was on the second floor, I quickly got back in. The woman could tell I was nervous and anxious and asked me if I was okay. Bumbling like an idiot I told her that I was really nervous because it was my first time wearing the headscarf.

Her response came like a slap in the face, "Well, you Muslim women are all oppressed aren't you." She said it with such venom and in such a patronising way I nearly cried my eyes out.

But then I had this strange feeling of calm come over me. I felt as though the lift had turned from a box closing in on me to one of the corn fields I used to run through back home. There was so much air to breathe and the light in the lift had turned into sunlight. I replied to her in a nice, polite way, "Not oppressed, no. Just dealing with ignorant people, one person at a time."

That was the first of many similar occasions, I've lost count how many. I didn't understand the amount of problems my new religion would cause. Having chosen Islaam, I never guessed it would cause such interest from friends, colleagues or the media; I didn't anticipate the depths of loneliness I would feel, or the division and isolation it would create.

I never imagined that someone's faith was of so much importance to other people. I had always thought, obviously very naively, that a person's faith was between them and God… oh how wrong I was! Becoming a Muslim was apparently everyone's business, Muslims and non-Muslims alike. I am no longer myself but the property of many.

But I guess I should start my story at the beginning. So let's rewind…

TWO

INNOCENCE, LOVE, LOST

My earliest memories are with my father. I remember walking along West Street, Long Sutton holding his right hand with my left, and swinging my blue bag in my right hand. I treasured that little bag because it had the words 'Daddy's little girl' on it. I felt the sun on my face and I remember skipping along beside him. There was also a cool breeze. I was really happy and blissfully unaware of how this day would become one of the most treasured days of my life.

Sitting on a stool next to the bathroom sink watching my father spread shaving foam across his face with a barber's brush was enchanting. I was waiting for him to look at me, to smile one of his playful smiles and of course to dab a little of the foam onto my nose. Would he do it? Sitting there waiting and watching at the way he moved the brush so smoothly and quickly fills me with joy even as I sit and type these words. I have a smile on my face and as I remember him dab a little foam onto the end of my nose, remembering how I giggled, the smile breaks into a happy grin from ear to ear. I loved my father so much, and thanks to God, we have had the opportunity to rebuild our relationship over the years, despite the best efforts of my mum, my dad (step-dad) and the court-rooms.

These two memories with my father are from the age of three or four.

No later because my mum decided her marriage to him was over, which also meant the relationship my brother, sister and I had with him, was also over.

I don't remember much else as a young child other than climbing trees in the park at the end of our garden. I would climb the trees with my brother Robert (Rob), much to his annoyance. He didn't want me around him, especially when his friends were with him. He is eighteen months older than me, and with hindsight, I can see our relationship has never been a great one. There are happy memories, but they are outweighed by some very unpleasant ones.

We were very lucky as children with the park in Long Sutton being an extension of our garden. Mum would allow us to walk across the park to school each morning as it was directly opposite our home. She could see us walk every step of the way. There was a lollipop lady who helped us cross the road into the school playground. Even though I could not see her smiling, I could see her standing at the end of our garden waving with Ellen, my baby sister by two years, sitting on her nonexistent hips.

The only thing she worried about was the man with the bike, 'the hunchback', who would be in the park at home time. I never knew why my mother, or the other locals, didn't like him. He never tried to speak with us, never came near us, he was just resting on his bike. He was an old man and he always wore a flat cap and a dark suit jacket. I remember him wearing bicycle clips on his trousers, which were proper trousers, an olive green colour. His bike was an ordinary black bike. There was nothing scary about him but Mum didn't want us to go near him, so I was always wary of him. Looking back now, I wonder whether it was just because he had a hunchback, and I wonder how upsetting and lonely it was for this man to be made an outcast and a monster in some people's eyes just because he was different.

My next memories are walking with Rob and Ellen to school in Emneth, where we'd moved to. I don't remember Mum taking us to school, but I do remember her picking us up from school every now and then. Seeing her at the school gates was magical and I remember running to her, but being told off if I ran too hard into her. She had been punched by a man once as she tried to stop him from hitting her friend Elaine. It had left my mum with problems with her neck and back. I remember being so proud of my mum when she later told me why she had these problems and I am positive this is why I am so loyal and protective over my friends. My mum is a strong woman and inspires me on many levels; yet our relationship has always been a distant one.

Rob, Ellen and I never got to spend much time with our father. We would wait for him to arrive at around 12:30pm every third Saturday. We'd travel back to his house, listening to the Beach Boys on the way; I'd be singing along with him, Rob and Ellen would be sat in the back. We would either visit the duck pond and Granddad Smith, or go and visit Nanny and Granddad Buffham. There would always be a Knickerbocker Glory at Dad's for us and as I got older he would allow me to make the dinner, something I either did alone or we did together. I don't really remember much about what Rob and Ellen did, although I do remember them watching TV and Rob sulking a lot.

I also remember us going to the park in Holbeach, where father lived, playing on the slide, walking around the park, going to the museum in Wisbech a few times (much to Rob's annoyance). I also remember a trip to Food Giant where he bought us all stationary for going back to school. When we got back home excited about our presents, it was short lived by the upset my mum created because we were 30 minutes late back. I remember thinking, we hardly get to see him, and you get us the rest of the time, why are you so mad at him? There was lots of traffic, why are you so nasty to him all the time? To this day, I still don't understand why Mum was rude to him every time we arrived home. There were times I would just wish my father would come upstairs to my bedroom and look at all my school work, to play all our records to him, on the super fast speed because they always sounded better that way. Why could our father not just join us all for dinner and a cup of tea? Why could we not be with him whenever we wanted? Why could he not come and see us whenever he wanted? Why was he not allowed to phone the house or come to parents evening at the school?

She never mentioned him to us, and she never asked us if we wanted to see him. He wasn't allowed to call the house to speak with us, so our relationship with him died out. Sometimes I wonder whether she regretted having the three of us with him, we were just a constant reminder to her of the failed marriage she had with him, and seeing him every three weeks could not have been easy. I know she loves us and did what she thought was best. I also know she had her own challenges, but I can't help wondering why seeing our father was not good for us. He never abused us, wasn't a junkie, or a drop out. He wasn't a criminal, he wasn't, and isn't a bad person, he was just the wrong man for her. But he was, is, still our father.

THREE

HAPPY FAMILY, BLOODY FOREIGNERS

I think many of the insecurities many others and I have, stem from my parents splitting up. You lose your safety net. The world is not as it should be anymore. The pain you feel is like no other you can describe.

I always believed I wasn't good enough for my father and it was my fault he left. If only I had been a better daughter, been a good girl, been Martin James, my mum's second child that never made it to this world alive, then maybe they would not have stopped loving each other.

I remember hearing so many times from the neighbours and a particular aunty that I had the energy and confidence of both Martin and I, and I used to hate it. Just because Rob was quieter than me did not mean I had somehow taken on my dead brother's persona. This is who I was. I was bright and bubbly. I was cheeky and playful. This is who I am meant to be, but somewhere along the way, I started to resent who I was. If I became the opposite of who I am, then maybe they would stop saying it. And sure enough they did. Eventually.

Otherwise, growing up in Emneth for the duration of my primary school life was so much fun. We would go next door and visit Nanny Aggie and Granddad George. They were not our real grandparents but they were wonderful people and so kind. We would spend hours with them, playing for hours in their garden with their little dog, a Bichon

Frise, called Fred. He was like a little cloud, so white and fluffy. They used to give us treats, tell us off if we were naughty and I know that Mum appreciated the times they allowed us to play in their garden as it gave her time to get on with the housework, or just have time for a coffee by herself. It took me years to realise the tiredness my mum must have been experiencing. She worked hard for us all. She always made a home cooked meal, we always ate together as a family and out of all my friends' mums, she was the most fun. She would play with us, bake with us and when she laughed I remember thinking it was the most magical sound in the world. My mum was happy again, and we'd soon find out why. She would allow us to run up the road to Betsy's Pad, a footpath by a dyke which ran from Hawthorne Road, the road we lived on, to Church Road. It's a strange name for a footpath I know, but that's country folk for you.

At the start of the path, in the end terrace house lived Brenda. She was a short woman with a mass of curly black hair. Although she was fierce, she was also kind. She would watch out for us from her windows, and on some days if we were really lucky, she might sneak us a biscuit as a treat. We would play paper trails along the pad, we would hide from one another and sometimes when we knew the farmer wasn't looking, would run along the edge of his field, that was until Brenda spotted us and hollered at us. Sometimes we would meet Jack, the neighbour who lived four houses down from us towards Brenda's. He would always give us Jacob's Cream Crackers. He lived alone and always wore a flat cap and rode his bike everywhere. I don't think anyone ever came to visit him, but I liked him. He always smelt of tobacco, either from his pipe or from his roll ups. It was a nice smelling tobacco, not like the smell of Mum's cigarettes. I always said if I started smoking, Superkings were not the brand for me. They smelled awful. It was the only thing I didn't like about cuddling Mum, the smell of her cigarettes.

The most fun we had was playing with Neil and Alison. They were brother and sister. Neil was a year older than me and Alison was a year younger. Their grandfather had a large garden and I used to love playing with them. I would also use Betsy's Pad to visit my friend Amanda. She was my first proper friend and had an older brother called Adrian. They used to argue and wrestle, and it was nice to know Rob and I were not the only brother and sister who argued with each other. They always ended their arguments in a nicer way than we did though and I always wondered if that was because their mum and dad were still together. It was nice having friends whose parents were still together, it felt safer.

By this time I remember Dad started to visit more, well the man who was to become Dad. I remember Mum giggling in the kitchen whilst we were doing jigsaws or watching TV. Whenever we heard her giggle one of us would sneak a peek to see why. It would be because Dad had been kissing her on the neck, standing behind her with his arms around her waist whilst she was making dinner. Sometimes we would hear her call out, "Roger!" because he had just pinched her bum. We would all giggle and he would come in and wink at us all. He brought a lot of happiness to our home and Mum wasn't as tired anymore. Things that needed doing around the house were either fixed or painted, the garden was kept neater and tidier and he had started to join us at the dinner table. We were a family again and I started to feel safe again. I don't remember Mum and Dad getting married, not even when I look at the photos, but I do know that I was the one who first started calling him Dad.

I also remember not long after they were married we were all given bikes. This made Betsy's Pad even more fun! Not to mention the whole village. We would ride our bikes everywhere. I even remember riding my bike once to my mum's friend Jane's house. She had a younger brother called Daniel and a daughter called Katy, who I would eventually become a babysitter for, along with Ellen. If truth be told, I had the biggest crush on Daniel ever. It lasted for years, even after I had my 'first love' and into my college years. The 'crush' though turned into me just wanting to have Daniel as a friend, as a big brother, because Rob just wasn't interested in being my brother. Daniel used to look out for me more than Rob. For some reason Rob just didn't seem to care. I was an annoyance to him and this became even more obvious when we moved from Emneth to Friday Bridge, three miles away.

Friday Bridge itself was the perfect place for me. Where we lived, we were surrounded by farms. We could go walking and cycling for miles. Nanny and Granddad lived down Maltmas Drove, along with Uncle Cyril and Aunty Fanny, Uncle Hugh and Aunt Daisy. They took up the first three houses. Carrie and her brother Danny lived in the fifth house, George 'the German' lived in house number eight and then there was

Maltmas Farm where Dad, Rob and I would go pheasant shooting on a Sunday. I loved pheasant shooting, and I still love shooting to this day, except I shoot clays now, not birds. There are only eight roads in Friday Bridge and I have cycled my bike from one end of them to the other countless times. In between all of them are fields, small ones, large ones and on every road we have the brothers and sisters of my Granddad Bates. Everyone in the village knew we were Rose and Bob's grandchildren and everyone in the village were either lifelong friends of my grandparents or related to them. I felt safe in Friday Bridge. With the farming lifestyle, endless fields and very few cars, it was a peaceful place to grow up.

I loved becoming a member of the Bates family. The Bates family homes were some of the best places to be, especially Nanny and Granddad's and Aunt Bet and Uncle Jack's, double especially at Christmas time! Christmas Day would be at Nanny and Granddad's. We would all help Granddad get the vegetables from the garden Christmas Eve, and then Mum and I would help Nanny with the lunch preparations. I was blissfully unaware of what Rob, Ellen and Dad were doing but I would always catch a glimpse of Granddad asleep in his armchair in the kitchen. Aunt Bet would start baking from November and her baking was the best, next to my Nan's. Aunt Bet, like Nanny, also taught me how to bake and cook and I treasure every moment I spent with them in their kitchens. Aunt Bet and Uncle Jack would invite every member of the Bates family over for Boxing Day tea. I remember the first time we went, I had never seen so many people in one house before, and neither had I seen so much food! And the best part we were allowed to have anything we wanted! When you were in Aunt Bet and Uncle Jack's house, so long as you were not greedy, rude or naughty, and so long as you enjoyed yourself, you could have and do what you wanted. Playing with Lucy, their little dog, was a lot of fun, but made me miss Lady and Sally, our two dogs who I knew were at home waiting for us to return.

Nanny had the biggest kitchen and the cupboards were always filled with goodies. Her treacle tarts were just the best! The pastry just melted in your mouth and the treacle just flooded your mouth with the sweetest taste. Never have I ever had a treacle tart like Nanny made, or anything that comes close to it. We would bake most weekends. Cakes, every kind of jam tart you can think of; we'd make jam, coconut jam tarts, lemon curd tarts and she would always have a stash of peanut cookies and custard creams for Mum and me. Dad would have his Rich Tea biscuits, Rob and Ellen would have their chocolate digestives and every Saturday night when we stayed over, Rob and Ellen would have a cup of Milo with their biscuits and I would have hot milk. Ellen and I would sleep in Dad's old bedroom and Rob would sleep in the third bedroom. On the Sunday, after Nanny and I had made lunch, Rob and Ellen would go home and I would cycle with Nanny to see her sister Alice in Strathmore House. Afterwards we would cycle somewhere else for miles, returning in time to have sandwiches for supper with Granddad. Granddad would then walk me to the top of Maltmas where the playing fields were, I would then carry on walking to the main road, turn around and see him still standing there with Suey, the little whippet dog he and Nanny had. I would turn around and wave, see Granddad put his hand up in the air and then he and Suey would walk back to Nanny. Suey went everywhere with them pretty much, even on holiday to Caister Sands when we went one year together as a whole family.

I would spend hours after school with Nanny in her kitchen baking and cooking and at weekends. I'd spend hours in the garden with Granddad planting and picking vegetables, learning about how everything grew, when to plant things and when to pick them. I'd walk with Granddad and Suey, up and down Maltmas Drove and around Needham farm, not really saying anything, just being together with the odd sentences thrown in. He'd tell me about the farms, the crops and come out with sayings such as, "If you can make someone smile, then it's worth waking up." I felt at peace walking with Granddad and sitting with him and Nanny out the front of the house in the garden. It was nice being surrounded by fields on all sides. My mind could just wander and absorb the world around me. Everything was peaceful.

Being surrounded by the open fields watching the farmers work hard and seeing how much effort everyone put into working gave me a strong work ethic. Mum and Dad worked really hard, Nanny and Granddad worked into their seventies, as did many others in the village. I decided I wanted to work and got a job at the post office delivering the morning papers. I had to get up early and cycle three miles every morning to deliver them. It was Dad who woke me up most of the time. He would get in from work after working all night at Spillers, have a cup of tea and then come upstairs to wake me up. Fridays and Sundays were the worst days; that's when the magazines and supplements came out. I enjoyed the time by myself thinking about things, watching lights come on, hearing the tractors already chugging away in the fields. The open spaces were perfect for my imagination to fill the empty spaces with thoughts and questions. On the really wet and snowy days, Dad would drive me around, and then when we got back, I would have breakfast, get ready for school and Mum would take us. Mum and Dad worked as a team and they just did what needed to be done. You knew that they would never break up. You also knew that when Mum said no to something, you never went and asked Dad, or vice versa. They were a united front and we knew it.

As I reached the age of high school, my imagination grew and ideas started to take place in my mind of a bigger world and different ways of living. The possibilities of life started to excite me. Meeting the other pupils from other schools, learning about a world bigger than my own, I started to daydream more and more. At primary school in Emneth, I had been reading books from classes two years ahead of me, and now I was at high school, I was devouring more and more books. The library was my favourite room in the whole school. Books on every subject and I wanted to read them all. I'd have four or five books on the go at once to make sure I never lost interest in reading. The only drawback to reading so much was the comments that started to be made by my mum. Having encouraged me to go and look in one of my books, she was now coming out with comments such as, "Know your place," and, "Do not get ideas above your station."

This is where I made my first mistake. I *did* get ideas 'above my station' and I would dream of a life in a bigger house, just like Townsend House on the Elm High Road, I loved that house. I only saw it from the outside, but I always wanted it. I knew it had a large enough garden at the back, and a drive at the front with large tall trees. I loved everything about it, the brickwork, the windows; the traditional feel of it. I so desperately wanted to go inside it. I would look at it every day on the way to school and back. I never saw anyone come or go, I never knew who lived there or what it was like inside. I just knew it was a nice size family home and just like the one I could see myself living in. The only problem was, it was in Elm and, "People like us didn't live in Elm."

It was around about this time that I really started to notice the resentment between the locals and the 'foreigners' that came to the International Farm Camp. I started to take more notice of the workers at the Camp. I would go for a bike ride and if I saw one of them I would ride over to them and say hello and start talking with them. Finding out where they were from and what their homelands were like, and why they had come to Friday Bridge. I wanted to know what they ate. I wanted to know so much about them, I even asked them if they believed in God. I didn't see it as the loaded question it is nowadays. I spoke with so many of the farming students from the camp and they were nice. I mean really nice. They told me what they were doing at the camp, about their families and about their plans for the future. They inspired me to think about my future and what I wanted. They taught me that it didn't matter what your passion was, so long as you followed your heart. They taught me to travel the world and meet people because it was a fun and interesting thing to do. They told me they came to work, to study and to learn about England. They wanted to learn a new language and culture. The way in which they spoke about their lives, aspirations and their travels inspired me. I had never heard anyone from the village speak the way they did. No one I knew wanted to leave the area. No one spoke of dreams and aspirations.

I started to learn words from their different languages and even started to make up sentences and pretend to have conversations with people in my 'new language'. I even got my little sister hooked on conversations in my 'new language'. Mum and Dad were not happy. Not only could they not understand a word either of us were saying, it also made them aware I was talking to these foreigners.

I was always told not to speak with them because they could not be trusted and it was not safe. When I questioned why it was okay to trust them to work on the farms but not to speak with them I got more standard responses such as, "Because they will fill your head with funny ideas," and, "Because they are different."

Why is it so bad to be different? Surely, we are all different? My experience with them was so far removed from the perceptions that most of the villagers had of them I just could not believe anything bad I was told about them. The continued conversations I had with the students started to cause a lot of trouble at this point, mainly because I became aware of a world outside of my white English family, the 'white English' being something that had never occurred to me before. I was told to stop talking with them. I could get kidnapped and taken off anywhere! To me, being taken away from Friday Bridge for a big adventure to some far distant land sounded just perfect. It was all the encouragement I needed to talk with them more. I could fall in love with a tall dark handsome stranger and be whisked away overseas (How these young girl fancies pan out hey!) Looking back now as a mother myself, I understand the fear my mum and dad had, of me, their daughter, being kidnapped by a stranger. But I know *anyone* could do it, not just those 'bloody foreigners'.

FOUR

GOD? DON'T ASK

Growing up in my family, religion was never discussed. Ever. (Neither was politics, but that's for another time!) My family only attended Church when there were weddings, funerals and christenings, pretty much I guess like most families I knew of back then. I would always wonder why we would go to these events if we did not believe in God. Surely to enter God's 'house' you actually had to know Him and believe in Him? Religion, my mum and dad would argue, caused too many wars and even more problems. I never understood this, because if God had created us, as we were told He did at school and when we went to christenings and funerals, why would a loving God have created religion for us to kill and fight with each other. It just didn't make sense. So I would ask, "Why does it?"

Only to receive the standard replies, "Because it does. Now stop asking questions."

I wanted to know further still why I was not allowed to ask questions, and why I never seem to be given the answers I was looking for. I learnt as I grew up that to question the church or my parents was a bad thing. But my mum also told me, "If you don't ask, you don't get!"

Life was very confusing.

I wondered if anyone else had the same questions as me, did everyone answer the same questions with the same answers. Surely someone somewhere had the answers to my questions, I was only a young child and adults had all the answers… didn't they?

At this stage there were only two times there was anything to do with religion in my life:

The first was the Sunday evenings Rob, Ellen and I would spend at Nanny and Granddad Bates' home. We would watch "Songs of Praise" with good old Harry Secombe and Thora Hird, God bless 'em![1] Believing in God seemed to be only for the old people and the 'nicely turned out' families… maybe it was only for the posh and the old then. Maybe that is why my parents didn't have the answers.

The second time was when I was at Brownies. The girls and I would have to clean the local church every other week 'To do our duty to God' – and no doubt so the Brownies could get a very big reduction in the cost of hiring the church hall, or am I too cynical? When I asked why we had to clean the church to do our duty to God, I was met with, "Because cleanliness is next to Godliness," or the usual, "Stop asking questions and just get on with it." So, getting close to God meant not asking questions and cleaning!

This kind of thinking continued over into Girl Guides and I just had to say, "Er, no thanks. Not really my thing." Unsurprisingly I was asked to leave the Guides years later for being 'insubordinate' to the Guide Leaders and a very bad girl. Becoming a rebel seemed to be a reoccurring phase I was going through at home and now it was spilling over into the Brownies and Guides.

So far my dealings with this God business are not that endearing and to be honest I was really confused. Why would my Grandparents and older relatives, teachers at school and all those 'nice posh people' on TV believe in something that meant you were not allowed to ask questions and you had to clean all the time?

I remember being given a Book of Psalms by the school, and having a Bible with the thinnest of pages, maps of Arabia and pictures of "Jesus" and the "disciples" in it (I've put the words Jesus and disciples in quotes, as I now realise the pictures were complete fabrications, we don't know what they looked like, and it's safe to say they didn't look blonde, as they were all native Palestinians). I used to hide both of them so Mum and Dad couldn't find them or tell me off for reading them. I am not sure whether they were cross at me for reading the Bible and the Psalms or just because I was reading in bed when I should have been sleeping; either way, they didn't like it. They didn't like me watching *Highway to Heaven* either on a Sunday morning with Michael Landon, but I loved it. The Waltons and the Clampetts also went to church and believed in God, but they weren't 'posh' people. Yes, they were TV characters but surely there was something in it all. There were also many churches everywhere; that must mean something?

My love of reading was taking off at this point and I was always searching for the next big adventure or reading the Bible or my Book of Psalms. I was finding the more I read the more questions I had, the more places I wanted to go to. My mum invested in a set of Disney Encyclopaedias and I loved each and every one of them, although I think my mum sometimes wished she had never bought them. They only increased my incessant ability to ask questions. The more I read the more I wanted to know. The more I wanted to know the more I learnt, the more I learnt the more I wanted to learn. Rob had a keen interest in nature and used to read the nature based books or he'd escape upstairs to his room and play on his Amstrad CPC 464 computer. He'd want to play Football Manager and I would want to read the text book and try out the coding described in the endless pages. He would have none of it and so we played Football Manager. He was Kenny Dalglish, manager of his beloved Liverpool FC, who he still supports to this day, and I would be the dreaded Manchester United, the arch enemy. A team I came to support later through the years, which then died off after I discovered raving.

Because I was always sat with my head in a book, I would rarely hear Mum call us for dinner. Many times she would shout at me, "Dawn Louise, will you get your head out of that book and come to the table for dinner!" Simply because I had not heard her the first three times. I would walk around the house reading, lie in the garden reading, go to bed reading, my head was constantly in a book of some sort. I even took up writing a diary which was great as I could make up my own stories and record how I was feeling, questions I had, thoughts I pondered over and adventures I wanted to have. One of those adventures was to visit Palestine, the land of Prophets described in my Bible. I wanted to learn more and more about God and the messages he had sent to us through all the Prophets. Whenever I had a question, Mum would say, "I don't know, go and look in one of your books." Needless to say, the more she pushed me away into my books, the more she pushed me away from her.

My relationship with my step-dad has on the whole been a good one. He has been my dad since I was four, but I have never allowed myself to get close to him. I always felt guilty about having fun with Dad because I did not want my father to find out, but then I didn't want to upset my dad by having a nice time with my father, or talking about him and our times with him. I felt immense guilt about calling either one of them Dad whilst in front of the other. I always wanted to sit on one of their knees, have a hug and have them tell me everything would be okay. But it always felt wrong to do so. Mum would always accuse me of trying to come between her and Dad and to this day, I still have no idea why she would say such a thing. This made me hate having attention from my dad, even though I just wanted to have the freedom to be with him as any girl would want to be with her dad. I knew he could never be my father, so I bought him a fridge magnet once with the words 'Anyone can be a father, but it takes someone special to be a dad'. I wanted him to be someone I could turn to when the relationship with my father deteriorated. I wanted someone to protect me, and I know he did in his own way. But I never understood his way. I wanted him, and my father, to tell me that they loved me. I still do. Never once have I heard either of them say it to me. Dad just changes the subject, which I have just come to accept that declarations of love are just not the 'done' thing, and, my father, well, he is just not good at saying how he feels about anything. Since father and I have been in touch with each other again, he's opening up, we both are. But I know it will take time. He has been on his own for 28 years, a dad for less than 125 days over a 22- year period. The last six years that we have been in touch have been more about two adults getting to know one another, not as father and daughter. I know it will take time and, God willing, we will have that time.

I cannot recall a time when either my father or my dad sat me or my siblings down to explain things to us. No guidance as to how the world works or how to go about choosing and creating a future for ourselves. I remember Dad being there whilst I was looking over college courses, I remember him being there at parents evening and having a proud look on his face; but never him guiding me. He has a phrase he says a lot, "I dunno." I should really get him a t-shirt with it on for his birthday. He never says it with thought or reflection, just with a non-committed, lack-of- interest tone to his voice.

I remember watching the US sitcom *My Two Dads* and wishing I was the girl in it simply because the relationships she had with her two dads were good ones. I remember Mum not being overly happy that I enjoyed the show so much, but she never switched it off. Having two dads was not all it cracked up to be in my case, but don't get me wrong, I love them both for very different reasons.

Yet seeing my mum and dad be so happy together gave me faith in marriage. I would pretend to be a bride with Mum's net curtains. We had many happy memories as a child and if any of us say any different, then we are lying. Dad has provided us with a home and some really great holidays, not to mention the best Nan and Granddad ever! We had a good life. I have many happy memories of being on the beach fishing at Caistor and Yarmouth, not to mention many other beaches in that area such as Salthouse and Trimmingham. We used to go and watch Dad play football every Saturday and some Sundays, running up and down the side lines cheering him on. These are some of my best memories of him. I loved being on the farm with him too. He was so much fun and had so much energy. He would play rough and tumble with us all, wrestle with us but after he was made redundant things changed. He stopped playing football around this time too and took up river course-fishing. I hated being by the river bank. I always felt that this new hobby stole him from us. No longer were we allowed to cheer him on, even when he caught a big fish! No longer were we allowed to talk to him, it would scare the fish. He became boring to me. I wanted to talk to him. I wanted him to run about with us, pick us up and turn us upside down. I wanted my fun dad back… but he just wanted to sit by the river, being quiet and waiting for a float to disappear or the sound of his beeper on his carp rod to go off. Rob and Ellen enjoyed coarse fishing. I hated it. I disappeared into my books. My books were my escape. I could be Nancy Drew[2] off on an adventure to solve a crime, pretend to be Katy[3] or one of the Famous Five! I hated fishing unless it was on a beach… then I could be as noisy as I wanted. When we were on the beach, the fun dad returned. If we were at Weybourne Beach, he would chase us up the beach and put stones down our trousers. At every beach he would pretend to throw us in the sea, it never failed to amuse us.

On some of the beaches we would run around in the sand dunes and hide. We would always have our moon boots on. We would always have egg sandwiches or thickly cut red Leicester cheese sandwiches with tomato sauce; all on white bread. There was always a flask of tea, Mum hated coffee in a flask. And there was always sand in the sandwiches… I remember my sister asking once if that was why they were called sandwiches, well it seems logical doesn't it?

Spending so much time on the beach as a child with so many happy memories has given me a lifelong love of the beach. I love it at any time of the year, preferably when it is cooler and with fewer people on it. The beaches in the UK in winter are my favourite because it reminds me of night time beach fishing with the 'tilly lanterns' and sleeping on the beach watching the moon as I fell asleep. It reminds me of our October holidays at Blue Sands holiday cottages in Caistor on Sea, a place I long to return to with my boys and my mum and dad.

I love all three of my parents, my brother and my sister so very much. I have fond memories of them all; it is just a shame that our relationships with one another are not as happy now as they once were.

---

1. My Nanny's favourite hymn was "The Old Rugged Cross" and even now when I hear it, I hear her singing with all her heart. Even to the point that several years after she passed away, when I was maybe five or six months pregnant with Khaalid, my first child, I heard the first few bars and burst into tears. (I was very hormonal and very close to Nanny) My husband thought there was something wrong with the baby and panicked for quite a few moments. He was very relieved to realise it was me just being sentimental, something he has got used to, had to get used to! I can see Nanny

now… sitting in her armchair, or peeling vegetables with me beside her at the sink, singing her heart out. She was a great woman and her faith in God was strong. I wanted what she had.

2. From "The Nancy Drew Mystery Stories"
3. From "What Katy Did Next" by Susan Coolidge

FIVE

SCHOOL DAZE TO COLLEGE RAVE

High School was the worst time of my young life. I started taking drugs[1] in the form of alcohol at home. We were allowed a glass of wine on special occasions. Mum and Dad both smoked cigarettes and so the passive smoking made me accustomed to the smoke. I got caught smoking herbal fags5 with Yvette and Theresa in the school toilets, for which I was nearly arrested for stealing the cigarettes, simply because the shop owner Mr Hardy refused to believe his staff had served me with them in the first place. Luckily I had the receipt and instead of him calling the police like he intended to do, he dropped the issue; smart move I'd say.

I never really had a set group of friends at school. I sat, talked, and hung out with everyone, but I never allowed anyone close enough to me, as I thought they wouldn't really like me and then they would just leave anyway. The legacy of my parents splitting up. I never felt confident that people really liked me; my thinking was they were just being nice to me, so it was easier to hang out and have fun than to open up and share secrets. I didn't like myself due to it being my fault for Dad leaving, there was obviously something wrong with me because my brother didn't like me, and Mum regularly told me that she may love me but she didn't like me very much. Plus I was still haunted by the comments of only being outgoing due to having my dead brothers persona as well as my own, so what was left was a lot of self hatred.

When the teasing started by the boys at school, the 'in crowd' of girls at school took it upon themselves to take the teasing to a whole new level. With Michaela and Helen leading the way in the bullying, everyone else in their crowd started to follow suit. I remember coming up against Michaela on the netball court when we were in primary school. I was wing defence and she was wing attack, she couldn't get past me ever and although it was a position not many people wanted, I made wing defence my own, just like I did with first base in rounders. When we met at Marshland High School, she made it her personal mission to make my life hell. My clothes were not good enough, I was too fat, too ugly, too boring and I had a boy's haircut. There were other girls I really liked, but I always seemed to be a third leg, just getting in the way. Tracey had Leanne, Dotty always had Lisa H or Lisa T. Lisa T threatened me on more than one occasion to stay away from Dotty, in the end, it was either be bullied by Lisa and her gang from the Queens School, as well as Michaela and Helen at Marshland, or just step away from Dotty. It was a hard choice to make, and I missed Dotty loads, but it saved having my hair pulled, being punched and more nastiness being heaped on me every time I went into town. Tracey, Leanne, Dotty, and Lisa H were always kind and lovely to me; I just wish I'd had more of a chance to trust them.

The only one I felt I could trust at school to be there for me was Jaime. She was, and still is, a very dear friend. I love her and her mum Sandra very much. Friday nights I would go home with Jaime from school or Dad would drop me off at her home later on. We would get ready to go out, listen to Diana Ross and Cher as we got ready, not the coolest of music but we didn't care. We would be singing and laughing, annoying Nigel her older brother who was way too cool, but he was never rude or nasty. He would tease us in the way I could only dream my brother would. Jaime's family was to me what a family should be. I loved the way they all talked with each other, teased each other and loved each other. They made me feel so welcome and like part of the family, that when I had to leave to go home, I would be sad I was going home to what would more than likely be another argument. The arguments and the snide comments were reasons I never invited friends home, and the reason I wanted a job in the evenings.

Turning 14 had been a blessing because I got a job on a Thursday, Friday and Saturday working at the local Fish and Chip shop. It gave me extra income too, so I could spend money on whatever I liked, namely alcohol when I finished work and met Jaime and the girls in town Friday night. I also started buying makeup to make myself look older. I was already physically developed, so the makeup was just what I needed to be able to get served at the bar, some four years earlier than was legal. Never once was I asked for identification.

I drank copious amounts of alcohol from the age of 14 in the White Lion and the Rose and Crown. I remember finishing off half a bottle of JD (Jack Daniels) one Friday night and staggering across Freedom Bridge on the way back to Jaime's house… but we ended up in the Red Lion and I really don't remember the rest of that night at all. It did involve some loud singing and Jaime's brother Nigel shaking his head at us when we arrived. This was a regular Friday night occurrence. The alcohol numbed the pain I was feeling inside.

When I went home I could hide the fact that I was bulimic by saying I had eaten at Jaime's, and at Jaime's I could say I had eaten before Dad had dropped me off or Jaime and I would eat when we went out. When I wanted to purge the food at home, I would walk to the bottom of the garden and hide behind the conifers, throwing up over the fence so Lady and Sally, our two dogs, wouldn't be able to eat it. Either that or I would wait until Mum and Dad had gone to Nan and Granddad's with their shopping, or to give them the increasing amount of medication they had both started to take. Rob was always in his bedroom, Ellen was in our bedroom and the toilet was downstairs near the front door, the furthest point from the bedrooms. It was also the best place to know when Mum and Dad arrived back because I would be able to hear them open the gates at the end of the driveway and the car pull in. Plenty of time to flush, wash my face and hands and start making them a cup of tea, as well as eat a little bit of toothpaste. Shortly after I had begun purging, I began getting constipated, so Mum took me to the doctors who prescribed Senekot, the natural laxative. Well this was great, purging and taking laxatives! The weight was soon coming off. With the weight loss, some of the teasing stopped. With Jaime's ever increasing friendship of me, some of the other girls started befriending me. Kym and Anna were the ones who were the nicest, the only problem I had with being around Kym was Michaela was her closest friend. Anna was like none of the others, she was arty, alternative and a breath of fresh air. Being friends with Jaime and Anna, things at school started improving. I was getting better grades and growing in confidence. The bulimia coupled with my hair now at shoulder length meant I no longer fitted into the names and nastiness that had been the cause of the bullying. There were only two boys at school I trusted and that was because they had stood up for me. Justin and Wesley were two of the coolest boys in school, and neither of them ever made me feel like crap. Justin was the new boy and Wesley, well he was just a really funny, kind, and cheeky guy. When Michaela started on me one day walking down the corridor from the music room to the library, Wesley and Justin told her to back off and leave me alone. I have never forgotten that day. That day they gave me the courage to speak up for myself. That day was also the day I wished my brother was the one that had protected me from it all. Little did I know he was also suffering from name-calling. Knowing what I knew about what was going on at home with the teasing he got from Dad for being tall and thin, and the name calling he had at school, I wish I had understood more, but Rob is a closed book. He just took it and said nothing, the rage building up inside of him ready for it to explode many years down the line.

Things at school were getting better and I had started to take a keen interest in religion and science. Miss Eddon taught religious education, Mr Baddeley taught chemistry and physics and Mrs Richards taught biology and the natural world. I loved these lessons, although chemistry was never my strong point. Once we were all talking and Mr Baddeley had told us to be quiet many times. We were making the sulphur volcano and mine just was not working. Whilst he was busy helping others towards the back of the class, I threw my experiment in the bin ready to start again. Little did I know that it was working, just not as quickly as I wanted it to! I don't know who smelt the smoke first, but when I tried to tell Mr Baddeley, he kept telling me to be quiet. Flames started coming out of the bin and water didn't seem to put it out for some reason. Finally after many attempts to tell Mr Baddeley the bin was on fire, he listened.

Just in time too. Not only could I not deal with nearly setting the entire science lab on fire and having to deal with Mr McMullen the head teacher, I really could not do with the grief I knew it would cause at home.

Religious education class with Miss Eddon was the first time I heard about different religions. She was a devout Christian, and her belief in God was inspiring. Many of the other pupils that went to my school had, or showed, very little belief in God. It was not 'cool' to believe in God, so no one dared say they did, but one or two were clever enough not to deny it either. Having been able to avoid bullying for a while I was not about to admit I believed in God simply because of the teasing and bullying that went on if you did admit to it.

We learnt about many religions, mainly Christianity and Judaism, but the ones that captured my imagination and my heart, also changed my life immensely. We were not taught much about the 'other' religions, just enough, but that small amount was enough for a whole new world to open up to me.

The 'other' religions were Buddhism, Taoism and Islaam, and I loved the idea of them all. They all connected with me on many levels: being moderate in our behaviour; being at peace; reflection and meditation; compassion; humility; being connected to nature and looking after our environment; being healthy and taking care of our bodies, our vessels, for this journey on Earth until we met with the Creator of all things. I didn't associate the bulimia with being unhealthy because this wasn't something spoken about. Being fat was unhealthy, smoking was unhealthy but not being thin, being thin was a good thing.

Buddhism seemed really cool, but I thought the monks were a bit selfish. Everyone paid for them to live their life, without them donating a penny to society. This went against my work ethic, and I wasn't really into the idea of worshipping a man so Buddhism fell by the wayside. I did understand that Siddhartha was a holy man, one that taught lessons of enlightenment following his 'escape' from Royal life into the streets of Kapilavastu (Olden day Nepal). I loved the Karma thought process that what goes around comes around, and how internal peace and external peace are linked. You are good and kind to others as you are for yourself and hey presto everyone should be happy. But there was just something missing and I could not figure it out.

Taoism was the second faith that connected deep within me. Not sure if that is because I am a farmer's daughter and was surrounded by nature all the time; but there is something deeply magical for me watching the seasons and the crops alter year in year out. Being able to see my food planted, watch it grow, see it harvested and then prepared for eating. Fishing on the beaches, shooting on a Sunday for Pheasants meant we caught the food, prepared the food and ate the food. I also got to choose which chicken we had for lunch sometimes, it was great. I loved it. I also loved the fact that Taoism promoted integrity amongst people, the use and understanding of energy and the natural elements such as fire, water, air and earth. It encompassed so much of my life; it felt like I was being hugged. I remember sitting on the beach hearing the crash of the waves, feeling the water on my face, the wind in my hair, the sand running through my fingers and the fire lantern giving us light late into the night. It all made sense to me. For us to be whole, we had to have, and use, these elements properly and in harmony.

It was learning about integrity of self and the energy forces both from Buddhism and Taoism that made me realise that making myself eat huge amounts of food to make up for the hunger and then throwing up wasn't the best idea I had had. I needed to stop doing it, and besides, my breath had started to have a strange smell and my jaw was really hurting. I was also finding it very hard to eat food that wasn't a bag of crisps or chips. They were small and gave me energy, something I was starting to lack and meant that sports at school were being affected. I was losing my places on the school teams and this was upsetting. I loved sport but just had no energy to participate properly. I knew I had to tell someone, I needed help to stop, I wasn't strong enough by myself.

Choosing to tell someone something when you have had too much JD and Coke or too many Gatsby's is not a great idea. You pick the wrong person or you just say something you will regret. I chose the wrong person. I chose Emma. She had been at the school for nearly a year and she had been coming to the pub with us for a while. I got on well with her and one night as we were crossing Freedom Bridge in Wisbech, I asked her if I could tell her something. She promised she wouldn't say a word, so when we got to the gardens on the other side by the Red Lion Pub we sat on a bench and she asked me what was wrong. I told her about the bulimia and told her I didn't know how to stop. She gave me a hug and said she would be there for me. It was the first time I had trusted anyone with anything, it's just a shame I was drunk and a shame Emma used it as a way to impress the girls at school. Waking up the following Monday felt good, I had broken through the trust barrier and felt that I had another friend. Walking through the school gates proved otherwise. Helen was stood near the gates and as soon as I walked in she started making vomiting noises. The others in her gang all started laughing and in the centre of the group stood Emma. I just looked at her and walked on through the group fighting the tears. There was no way I was going to allow them to see me cry; and there was no way I was going to confide in any one else either. From that moment on, I hated Emma, I hated Helen and all the others too. I distanced myself from pretty much everyone, unable to trust their intentions. I focused on my school work and the upcoming mock exams. I needed to pass them if I was ever going to leave this area, leave home and leave all the memories behind.

Forgetting about the bullies and focusing on school work again felt good. I was making plans for my future and deciding upon what I needed to do, and I was going to do it by myself. I could trust no one and so it was down to me to make things happen. Shortly after making this choice, we went on a 'mini pilgrimage' with Miss Eddon to this place – I can't remember its name – and we were shown different pilgrims on their journey to find peace with God. That's when I saw it. That's when I felt this feeling of weightlessness and inner peace. I felt faint and as though I wanted to cry, more of relief than sadness, I had this deep desire within me to go to this place where everyone wore white. I wanted to go to Mecca. I wanted to go on Hajj.

I remember going home that night as if it was last night. My mum was dishing up dinner as Dad was going to work, he had less than an hour to eat and get back into town. We were having shepherd's pie. I ran into the kitchen and said to Mum, "I want to go on Hajj, I want to go to Mecca." I said it twice.

My mother's reply was, "Go and set the table, your dinner is ready."

I was stunned. My mother had never heard of either and her response to me was, *go and set the table, your dinner is ready*. No question about where or what these things were, just an instruction to set the table, as this was yet another 'phase' I was going through. I realise now that my Mum was just in a hurry to get Dad's dinner inside him before he went to work, but this was a big thing for the young me, still is. I want to go to Mecca. I want to go on Hajj.

Science played a big part in my journey to the one God, our Creator. I would sit in science lessons at school listening to Mrs Richards and Mr Baddeley; learning about how the world and our bodies worked. I was often told off for daydreaming when in fact I was thinking about what they were saying. I was trying to connect all the dots in my head. Trying to make sense of all the questions I had and how they related to everything. How could man have created the Ions and all the molecules? How could man make the rain clouds? How could man make the planets balance in the way that they did? And how did man make the plants grow? There had to be something that created all of this, because man is still learning how to understand the world around us. This was when I started questioning the link between Jesus being God or simply a messenger and prophet of God. I believed he was a man, born to Mary with God's blessing and a prophet. He followed God's word but is not God. It even said so in my Bible, or had I not understood the passage correctly?

In many of Miss Eddon's classes she would say that Jesus was the son of God, and then in others she would say he was God. How can he be both? You are either one or the other surely? I also wondered why Jesus looked like people from England and not from Palestine, when in my Bible there were maps showing the different lands of the prophets, detailing how the different tribes were broken up and how Palestine was a sacred place. I wanted to go to this place Palestine. I wanted to walk the lands of the Prophets. I wanted to learn the history of these places and find the answers to my many questions.

My head started to fill with ideas of travelling the world, seeing all sorts of places and meeting lots of different people. I started to get really excited about seeing the world. The furthest we had ever been was Cornwall and Devon, and even though I loved both, they were just not as exciting for me anymore. I wanted to go on an aeroplane. I wanted to fly through the clouds – how cool would that be? I wanted a passport. I wanted to eat different foods and see different things. I felt like I was going to burst! I was energised and felt so alive. I produced a piece of work on Islaam where I had written the whole thing starting from the back of the book, writing every letter in every word back to front so it mirrored the right to left style of writing the Arabs have. I had never enjoyed a project so much. My work was shown to the class as an example of how to do a project. Miss Eddon had said she had been very confused when she first started reading it, and then had been nothing short of impressed. I couldn't help wanting the floor to swallow me, not because of embarrassment but because I knew this would only lead to more bullying.

Shortly after the project, we received our mock exam results. Although most of my results were either C or D with one B, this was not good enough for me. I felt I had failed. This was just too much for me. Later that night when I went home, I just felt empty. I just didn't know what to do. I wanted to go somewhere else, but how could I go anywhere? I just wanted to disappear from everything, from everyone. So I walked downstairs, found my mum's Co-codamol, emptied 20 tablets into my hand, grabbed the vodka from the cupboard and took the lot. I went back upstairs to bed and went to sleep.

I woke up feeling really sick and realised that I was choking, the next thing I know my dad was running in. He looked really scared, and went to put my dressing gown on me to take me to the toilets. That's when he found the blister packets. I don't remember much else, but I do remember being in hospital. I remember seeing Mum and Dad, but not Ellen and Rob. I remember sleeping a lot. I remember phoning Anna and Jaime, but I couldn't get through to Jaime or her mum. I got through to Anna and when I heard her voice, I froze. What was I going to tell her? Why was I calling? I just needed a friend and so I told her where I was and made her promise not to tell anyone. Anna kept her promise.

She restored my faith and we were friends for many years to follow. Then I slept. I felt peaceful. I had escaped, even if it was just for a while.

During the last year at school, I just focused on my exams, working in restaurants at weekends and the supermarket Food Giant. With all this work, I had more money and less time at home. I managed to get the grades I needed to go to college: This is where I discovered raving, 'Class A'[2] drugs and a huge library. For self-discovery, this is just what I needed. The books gave me information, marijuana gave me a creative mind I had never had, and shut off the negative thoughts, and raving allowed me to be the free spirit and dancer I had always been inside but was too shy to be on the outside. Taking drugs opened my mind further than any of the fields back home and became a solution to many of my problems.

I was already a heavy drinker towards the end of school and had started smoking the odd spliff[3] in the 5th year, so daily spliff smoking was to become the norm at college.

I had been accepted into the Advanced Management course in Hospitality and Catering, something that I knew would give me skills in all areas of business as well as teach me to cook. I knew Mum and Dad couldn't afford to send me to university so my dream of being a teacher was never mentioned, or the course applied for. If I was going to escape living at home, it would be easy to find a job far away in a hotel or restaurant until I had figured out what I really wanted to do. Plus I was earning more in tips than I was in wages by this time, because as with everything, I had to be the best I could be in the hope Mum and Dad would be proud of me. At college I learnt about more alcoholic drinks and had changed from the JD and Coke and the Gatsby's to a nice Pimms and Lemonade in the summer time or a Dry Martini and Lemonade. Baileys Irish Cream substituted milk in fresh coffee and a Snake Bite and Black[4] was also very refreshing … something my new friend Rachel had introduced to me one night after work at Food Giant. There was of course the evil 20/20[5] drink that those of us in the early '90s would have experimented with. How we managed to buy all this alcohol underage is baffling, and why 20/20 was sold as alcohol and not paint stripper I will never know, but it was the start of Alchopops[6], so thank goodness they were replaced by Bacardi Breezers… much tastier!

After a while feeling sick, being sick, a lack of memory and feeling rough for the next two days just lost its appeal. I just didn't want to drink anymore… so I did as most people who 'give up' drink do, I switched to wine. Yes wine, because a glass or two of wine is not really drinking, is it? It's civilised. It's healthy for you, especially if it's red wine.

I also saw the affects of alcohol usage from a different perspective when I worked in restaurants and pubs and it was not pleasant. People vomiting just reminded me of my purging, which had decreased by this time but hadn't stopped. I also got to see so many people becoming obnoxious and arrogant, the copious 'Friday Night Fights', infidelity due to drunkenness, and people becoming 'prostitutes in denial'. This is what I call people who after they have had a few drinks, wander off with a complete stranger to have sex, never probably knowing their name or, in some cases, what they even looked liked. I was disillusioned with alcohol and I saw more fights in a month of working just weekends in a pub than in all the years I have been raving[7].

Due to the nature of my course I got to work in various hotels and restaurants across the country. I worked in Eastbourne on the south coast and made a huge amount of money. I was shown a new way of life down there. People had money; and they spent it well at the business functions they attended. Seeing all those ladies in those beautiful dresses at the black- tie dinners, hearing all the amazing conferences, I knew I wanted to go into the world of business. I was learning how to manage a hotel, staff and understand the basics of business on my course, and I was learning so much from the conferences I was servicing and the conversations I was over- hearing whilst serving dinner. I would read the marketing material of the businesses, understand what they did, my only problem was, how did I get to be a business-woman?

Following a personal development workshop in one of the hotels I worked in, I decided to keep a diary and a journal. I started writing down all the ideas and thoughts I was having about my future. Making plans and setting targets with all possible ways to complete them excited me and smoking a spliff whilst thinking about it all made the ideas and possibilities even more creative than ever. My best ideas always came to me whilst I was stoned or, for some strange reason, whilst I was sitting on the toilet!

College life was turning out to be better than I had ever imagined. I met people from everywhere and it was great to be finally rid of the bullies from school. My friends Jaime, Anna and Kym went to the same college as me but did a different course, so although I saw them around campus, I never got to see them much. I remember the first day of college waiting for the bus, a guy came walking up to the bus stop wearing a black pair of boots, black jeans, a black hoodie and a black denim jacket. He had his walkman on and a nose piercing. I had grown in confidence away from the school environment by working and becoming good friends with Rachel and as soon as this guy stopped walking, I asked him, "Who do you think you are, the Grim Reaper?" with a cheeky grin on my face.

He looked at me surprised, then smiled with a twinkle in his gorgeous eyes and just said, "No." His name was Mark and he was to become my closest friend for many years. If I was not at Rachel's smoking joints and getting myself and her pet rat Marley stoned, then I was at Mark's. Spending the time with Mark and Rachel in their homes made going home to Mum and Dad's much better. I was 'studying' at Marks and staying over at Rachel's ready for work the next day.

It all made sense and it helped me deal with the increasing decline in my grandparent's health. Granddad was becoming really poorly and so I would go to Nanny and Granddad's instead of going directly home. I was hardly at home anymore, Rob had moved out, I was seeing less and less of Ellen and, as I write this, I am beginning to realise, I was not a very good sister to her. I didn't know how to be, my head was so focused on my stuff and leaving that I never gave her the time she deserved, and for that I am really sorry because I love her with all my heart.

During the day at college, Jo, a friend on my course, and I used to walk to the football field at the end of the road and get completely stoned with joints and homemade Buckets[8]. There's a lot you can do with an empty plastic drinks bottle, some sellotape and a plastic bag. We would go back to college, listen to the lectures and do the work. I found the course a little boring to be honest as a lot of what I was being taught was stuff I had already learnt working in the restaurants. This was just the theory to back up the practice, and I believed more in the practice than I did in the theory. This was something some of the lecturers were not keen on me pointing out during the lectures. The others on the course were a really nice bunch, except one or two of them who had brooms so far up their own backsides I'm surprised they could bend over to kiss the backsides of the lecturers as often as they did. Still I had developed a group of friends outside of the course and this is where I discovered another lifestyle I would come to adore, raving.

I had been to an open air party before, but I would say my friend's new friend Tammy and her friend Sara introduced me to the raves that I came to know and love. I had not really associated the open air party as a rave because they were not the things that were described on the news as raves. The raves that were on the TV news in the '90s that 'destroyed' farm lands and had 'violent' party-goers 'abusing' the police and neighbours were nothing like the 1000+[9] raves I have since attended. But as anyone with any common sense will know, you cannot always believe what you see or read about in the news. The people at the parties I went to had been invited by someone who knew someone who knew someone etc., and *had* permission to use the land by the land owner (just not the police) and were too 'loved up' to even think of throwing a punch or abusing a neighbour. They may have hugged them, and spoke a lot of rubbish at times – okay spoke a lot of rubbish *most* of the time – but never would they have been abusive. That is just not what the rave scene is, or at least *was*, about. We were there to meet with friends; party our backsides off to some 'most excellent' music; have a 'blow out' and 'chill out' with new and existing friends afterwards.

I remember my first rave with Tammy as if it was yesterday. We went back to her home after college, had dinner, went upstairs to her bedroom, Tammy put on her beloved Jungle music and showed me her silver CHIPIE trainers. She loved those trainers so much, and she cleaned them to perfection. She has the most amazing red hair which was curly, and the steadiest hand I have ever seen to apply black liquid liner to her beautiful eyes. Yes, I had found a friend in Tammy and I loved her immensely. I still do, and I'm still in touch with her today. She helped me through so much, she doesn't even to this day know how much. I remember being inspired by her, the confidence she had in what she liked, and who she was. I loved her artwork, her laugh and her ideas. She was larger than life, a total Jungle queen and a total babe. Now Tammy and I only really disagreed on one thing, Jungle music. I just did not get it. I like one or two of the tracks and I could understand dancing to it if you were completely stoned, but I had energy, and lots of it and not just because of the white powder called amphetamine, or billy as we called it then.

Our first rave together was at the Pleasuredome in Skegness, it had House music, it had Happy Hardcore and some other music playing in the chill-out room. It wasn't open to full capacity as I know it can be, but it was a great night. It was the night I took my first E[10], a Dove; and a dove of peace it was. All the upset I had been experiencing at home, all the insecurities I had felt all my life melted away, I danced and talked that night like I had never talked and danced before. It was wonderful. It really was ecstasy. Tammy I thank you from the bottom of my heart. You and your friends gave me a precious gift that night, you gave me the gift of a friendship that freed me, and your friends became my friends. We had many more nights of dancing, laughing and talking absolute rubbish to each other in total ecstasy over the next two years. I will never forget them… well, until I get old and senile!

With this new release from negativity I became a happier person, I had an outlet finally to let off steam. Smoking joints helped my creativity. Dancing whilst on ecstasy and/or billy I was becoming more confident speaking with new people by going to different parties. I met a new group who took me to Hyperbolic[11], at the Kings Lynn Speedway. It was here I discovered Techno[12]. Listening to Techno was as if someone had grabbed me by the throat, slapped me around the face, woke me up from a deep sleep and allowed me to listen to music for the very first time. It made me smile; it made me want to dance. It made me feel even more alive than I had done at the Pleasuredome. I remember Paul Grant, Mr Hyperbolic himself, walking past me on the first night I went, and with a big friendly smile on his face he asked me, "Why are you standing at the side? Why aren't you dancing?"

I had no answer because I was awe struck by the energy, the presence of this music that not only had the best beat I had ever heard, but some of the funniest samples as well. People were having a laugh with each other in a way I had never seen. There were phrases said to one another that would be thought of as insulting, but with the raving crews, they were just 'friendly banter', people having a laugh with each other. The Hyperbolic crew were like a big family, and they came from all over Norfolk, Cambridgeshire and Lincolnshire to be there, some from further afield. I had found my new raving home for the next few years and I made friends with a group of people who I later spent more and more time with. I saw and experienced things that bought both joy and great pleasure to my life, but made me question things on many more levels.

Then things went wrong. Two new crowds emerged, one that just wanted to be wasted on drugs all the time, and one that came from the pubs at closing time completely drunk. Neither understood the happy vibe and the banter between us all and just made trouble. These were the ones where raving wasn't about having a wicked time with each other, or loving the music. They weren't interested in looking out for each other, they just wanted to bring dirty drugs into the scene, make money and cause problems. The 'happy vibe' was not so happy anymore and a few people got busted for drugs and the 'happy family' started to fall apart. People wanted others to take sides. Something I have never really done. People wanted to bring you into their bitching and back-stabbing about others, I was not going to be part of it. I did get pulled into it a few times and had to step back. Some people didn't like it because I always spoke with those that had always been good to me, even if they were 'not in our crew'. I ended up with no 'crew', just raving; and that suited me fine. I still went out with Tammy, I still went out with others, and I still had a great time. We started going to some bigger raves such as Helter Skelter, and I thank God I did (you'll understand why later).

The reason I love dance music so is because not only does it stimulate every sense in my body, it crosses language barriers, as well as cultural and ethnic differences. Some of my friends who DJ[13], DJ all over the world; and not just the Western world either. They play their music in the Arab world, and since I have been involved with the Arab world, I can see why. Some of the traditional music with the drum beats is so similar to the Trance and Techno that I love, I find myself thinking it is new Techno/Trance tracks with an Arabic sample. Dance music has so few words, it is just beats and rhythms, just like a heartbeat, just like the natural flow and rhythm of the world around me. Dance music brings people together in a way that not many other forms of music do. The spoken word is a barrier for most pop music, rap, hip-hop, rock, etc., just like culture and socioeconomics are barriers to other music such as classical. How many council estate kids do you hear listening to classical? How many of the upper class of society do you hear listening to Eminem? Dance music transcends all of these because it is so versatile and has so many different styles, from House to Hardcore, to Trance and Techno, and of course Tammy's beloved Jungle.

In a rave I could be ALL of myself, just me, completely free to be all of me. There was total acceptance of who I was; I wasn't a disappointment, I wasn't a bad daughter, I was just Dawn: a badass dancer and the sweaty girl who doesn't care what she looks like, and at that moment in time doesn't care about anything other than letting all frustrations out of her system through her feet as they hit the floor. Surely it is better to do that, than argue with someone? A rave is the only place I have ever felt total acceptance of who I am and what I do. Probably because we are all so busy dancing our backsides off and having a laugh, on drugs or not. Most people inside the rave, and outside, could not tell if I was on drugs or not. My mother never could tell. Nights I would come in completely straight[14] she would accuse me of being on drugs. The nights I was totally off-it[15] she said she preferred me like it because it was good to see me happy. All of my mother's favourite photos of me are the ones where I am buzzing-my-face-off[16] and just goes to show that she doesn't really know me at all, and no one can normally tell if you are on drugs or not, unless you are completely hammered[17].

I remember reading in the college library one Monday after a pretty heavy weekend raving in Skegness, that it was Muslims that went on Hajj, and to be a Muslim all you had to do was believe in the one God, believe in His angels, and that Mohammad was the final Prophet. Believing in the one God and angels was easy. Believing that Mohammad was the final Prophet made sense having read the information I had on him. I had seen some of the passages of the Qur'aan that he had relayed to the people of Mecca after they were revealed to him via the angel Gabriel. Knowing that I agreed with those three things, I just assumed I was a Muslim. It wasn't earth shattering for me at that point. It was just accepting the facts and evidence that were put before me. I closed the books, went for a joint and then a lecture.

After the lecture, I went to the football pitch, made another joint, and lay there looking up at the clouds forming different shapes and floating by. I was thinking about all the information I had started collecting in my head. I was thinking about the fact that I was a Muslim. What does it mean to be a Muslim? Was I really a Muslim? How come there wasn't a water-over- the-head moment? Was it really just a belief in the one God and Mohammad being the final prophet? What other things would I find out? Did my life have to change? If so, how? What else would I find out through my questioning, through science and nature?

I had been vegetarian for about a year, something my Dad teased me about, but one night at work I decided I just had to have a piece of scampi, and the chicken dish my boss was making smelt divine. I wanted to eat meat again so I decided I would only eat fish and chicken from then on. Finding out that Muslims didn't eat anything from pigs wasn't really a problem as I had already decided not to eat pig due to a food science lecture a month earlier, so that was not going to be a problem; there were many other meats out there. I didn't really enjoy roast beef, it always seemed too tough[18], but I did love Mum's cottage pie and I loved roast lamb, so giving up one meat was not going to be a problem. I also remembered that in the Bible and the Torah, it said not to eat pig, as it is un-clean. As Samuel L Jackson's character, Jules, says in *Pulp Fiction*, "Pigs are filthy animals."

This was my first clear link, a light bulb moment, between science and God's word[19]; it was this that was the most striking thing for me at this point in my journey. I had already been replaying all the science I had learnt during school, reading science books and natural world books in the library at college. Sitting on the beach with my family whilst Dad fished wondering and figuring out the natural order of things, I felt as though so many things were starting to click into place. The Torah, the Injeel (original Bible) and the passages I had read in books about the Qur'aan all said pretty much the same thing. There was a domino effect.

It got me thinking about the way in which the seas, crops, energies, forces and our bodies worked. It sent my head into a spin even when I wasn't stoned!

Many times after having been out raving all night, and all weekend, I would lie down on the bed and think about the questions in my head, about my life and where I wanted it to go. I would think about the arguments at home and I would think about how the world was created, science, philosophy and my belief in God. I knew the arguments at home were due to my constant questions, me not accepting things and wanting more information which neither Mum nor Dad could give me. They were challenged by my dreams and my ideas, my desires to have more and due to the amount of insecurities both my mother and I had, and still have to this day. She feels she is not good enough for me and I feel as though I am not good enough for her. I know I was living a life she didn't understand, didn't want to understand. I was honest with her about taking drugs because I just didn't want to lie to her. To me lying to her was much worse than taking the drugs themselves, but it broke her heart to know her little girl was taking the very things that had recently been over the news due to a girl called Leah Betts dying from taking ecstasy.

What the media failed to report on though was the amount of alcohol Leah had drank that night and the amount of water that her mother had worried her into drinking for fear of dehydration. Leah actually died because she had too much water in her system[20]. I had the understanding, if you can't drink alcohol whilst taking prescribed medication, it's best not to drink it whilst taking Es, billy, or acid[21]. There were many who did mix drugs and alcohol, but most of us drank water, and not too much of it either. Water was for pouring over your head because you were dancing so hard and sweating so much. Coming-up[22] on a pill was a powerful sensation, and everyone was in tune with each other. If you were in the middle of the techno room surrounded by other techno-heads and you needed a sip of water, you only had to think about a sip of water and the person next to you was already handing you some water.

The more I read about Islaam the more it made sense to me. I loved the idea that everyone was equal before God and we were to be judged by him alone. I loved the fact that we were encouraged to question[23]. I had driven my parents mad by being one of those children who always asks why. Even to this day, I am still asking why. I hope I never stop asking why, because for me that will be the day I stop learning and when you stop learning, your mind dies.

I had at this point not been able to find a Qur'aan. I had been able to find passages of the Qur'aan, references to Islaam in books on religion at college, books on world religions. I had seen mentions of the Prophet Mohammad in various books about the world's greatest leaders, but even though I had not seen a Qur'aan or read it from cover to cover, I still knew I wanted to go to Mecca, to go on Hajj. I didn't know how to get there or what I needed to do to get there, but I knew I would get there. One way or another, I would go on Hajj, one way or another, it was going to happen.

---

1. Alcohol and nicotine are drugs like any other. From now on though, simply as a kind of shorthand, I will mainly use the word "drugs" to mean banned recreational drugs, as that's the common usage of the word and provides an easy distinction between legal and illegal. 5 A "fag" is a UK slang term for "cigarette", I don't know why.
2. "Class A" was a police classification of illegal narcotics, although we did joke that they were called "Class A" because they were the best class. Saying that, I didn't try out any of the dangerously addictive Class As like crack or heroin, just the fun party drugs.
3. "Spliff" is a UK word for "joint" i.e. a cigarette containing any form of marijuana, usually mixed with tobacco.
4. Equal parts lager and cider with a dash of blackcurrant cordial.
5. Some sort of cross between wine and port drink that was fruit flavoured.
6. Alcohol companies had the great idea of making alcoholic drinks that tasted nice, and so would appeal to younger people, and would be drunk like a soft drink i.e. a "pop" drink, hence "Alchopops".
7. The police have admitted to me many times — off the record of course — they would rather police a rave, there's no fighting, no abuse and it costs the tax payers less money in manpower.
8. Marijuana smokers were always coming up with ever-elaborate ways of smoking Pot. Buckets were a particularly effective way of getting a lung-full in one breath!
9. Oh yes, I've worked it out, I've actually been to that many raves. Here's the maths: 10+ years of raving, at least 2 raves a week for on average 50 weeks a year = 50 x 2 x 10 = 1000 minimum. I was surprised by the number as well!

10. Ecstasy i.e. MDMA in tablet form. I read once that over two million Es were consumed every weekend in England; it really was/is the party drug. Ever wonder why something illegal is so popular?
11. Or "'yperbaalak", if said in carrot-cruncher accent :)
12. NOT the chart "techno" of the time e.g. 2 Unlimited: "no no, no no no no, no no no no, no no there's nooo lyrics"
13. Not just play music, like a standard radio Disc Jockey, but beat mix tunes so that one tune flows into the next, and what we hear sounds like a continuous flow of music, twisting, and turning, taking us an emotional journey.
14. Not on drugs i.e. not under their influence.
15. Not only on drugs, but also at the peak of the drug's influence, in the sweet spot, in the zone, etc.
16. Had too many drugs, and have either lost touch with reality, or are physically sick.
17. Had too many drugs, and have either lost touch with reality, or are physically sick.
18. Though that might have been because of my mum's cooking!
19. I have to point out that, as a Muslim, I do not believe the current Bibles or Torah are God's word. How can I, when the human authors of those books are listed in the books themselves? The Injeel and Tawraah mentioned in the Qur'aan were God's word, but they've been lost. That's not to say the current Bibles and Torah aren't inspired by God's word, but there's so much human intervention in them we can't know which words are God's and which aren't.
20. So you could just as well say Leah's mother was the cause of Leah's death.
21. LSD
22. The feeling when the effects of the MDMA really started to kick in, a bit disorienting, as the mind is getting used to being in a new state of consciousness.
23. Most Muslims nowadays *don't* question, even though the Qur'aan clearly states we must. This blind obedience is mainly down to a misguided "respect" for our elders & "scholars", and from following false Hadeeth.

SIX

GRANDDAD - TOTALLY REST IN PEACE

Life away from home when I was with Rachel and Mark was good. Life at work was great, I was earning lots of money, being promoted and had just become the youngest trainee hotel manager in the international chain of hotels I was working for. They wanted to make it permanent but I had already decided I wasn't going to stay in hospitality. The business conferences and businessmen and women I had met had completely turned my head away from the industry. The constant advice I was getting from them all was, "Go into sales, you'd be great at it, and once you can sell, running your own business will be easier."

At home though, things were taking a turn for the worse. My granddad was hallucinating badly and we all feared it meant his time was soon. The irony of it all was I had started taking acid and was loving my hallucinations[1]. I loved the deep meaning-of-life conversations, but sadly for me there were not that many people around me at the time who wanted to talk about the same things I did whilst on acid. They were lovely people, most of them, and they meant a lot to me, but it was becoming apparent we had different paths to walk in life. Tripping[2] with them was still fun, mind. And one of the unexpected benefits of the migraines I'd suffered from was that I experienced visual auras, and this meant I could create colourful patterns to my heart's desire while on acid.

Visualising images and spending hours thinking about things were the best things about tripping.

Unlike my hallucinations, my granddad's hallucinations were disturbing. He would see the room full of rats running everywhere; he would hear gun fire and have flashbacks from The War. I remember him being on all fours behind the couch one day avoiding the 'incoming fire from the enemy,' with my nanny in the kitchen sobbing. I sat with her and made her a cup of tea as there was not much we could do with Granddad when he was like that. I had made sure the front door was locked and kept checking on him to make sure he was okay, and most of the time he would snap out of it, sit back in his chair and go to sleep. I would go and sit next to him and hold his hand, stroke his hair and give him a kiss before taking Nanny back into the lounge. Granddad would wake up knowing nothing of it, ask my Nanny, "You okay Rosie?" Then skip off to the toilet, as well as any man the age of 81 can, singing "ay ay ippie ippie ay ay," stop off in the kitchen to grab a biscuit, then he'd tell me to put the kettle on. Nanny would get out her knitting, Granddad would put the "hos racin"[3] on and within a few minutes he'd be asleep.

Nanny and I would look at each other, smile and drink the tea with our favourite peanut cookies. I would be sat reading, she would continue with her knitting and Granddad would be snoring. These are the moments I treasure because everything was how it should be. He wasn't hallucinating, she wasn't crying and I wasn't feeling alone, or scared or unwanted. My grandparents' home was the only place in the world I felt at peace. On the dance floor in a rave I was loved-up[4] and dancing, peaceful because of the drugs, but at Nanny and Granddad's, this was *real* peace, *real* love and *total* acceptance. This, to me, was heavenly.

Shortly after Granddad started to have the hallucinations, I started to feel really guilty about the things I had been doing and the amount of time I had been away. Why had I not spent more time with them? Why was I not making the most out of my time? I had to sort my head out, if not for me, then for my grandparents. They didn't know what I had been up to, they probably wouldn't have understood it if they had. Of the drugs I'd taken, even alcohol was never a big thing in our family. Nanny and Granddad didn't drink anything other than a drop of sherry at Christmas. Mum had a drop of brandy if we went to a 60s 'do' at the village hall or she'd have a hot toddy[5] when she came down with a cold, which wasn't often as she 'didn't have time to have a cold'. I can't even think what my dad drank because I never really saw him with anything other than a shandy. I know this is why my drug-taking was such a big shock to Mum and Dad. They just didn't understand it and the media didn't help matters either with the scare stories they ran.

The night before Granddad died was the night I came home from working down in Eastbourne on a college placement. I remember wanting to go straight to see him. Something told me that I was never going to see him again if I didn't go. I had forgotten they had moved to a new bungalow in Church Road so it felt a little strange not going down Maltmas Drove. When I walked in, I remember seeing his face and a smile break out. I started smiling too, but I was crying inside. He looked so weak and so ill.

Again, the guilt for having spent so much time away hit me. I was so angry with myself. I hadn't seen them for nearly two months. What kind of granddaughter was I having been away from him for so long, not helping him and Nanny. I was selfish, I was a mess. All the conversations and the special times we had spent in the garden and walking together came flooding back to me. I tried so hard not to cry in front of them. I told him I had missed him so much and I was sorry I hadn't been to see him in a long time. I sat next to him on the arm of his chair and hugged him so tightly and that's when he told me that he loved me and was so proud of me. It was at this point tears escaped but one look at Mum and a light shake of her head, I knew I had to hold it in. He tugged at my arm and I sat on his lap and gave him another big cuddle, told him about the placement I had been on, about the sea and a few of the things I had been doing. I wanted to tell him everything about what I was going to do, the things I wanted to do, all the things I had heard in the seminars but he just looked so tired. I knew he didn't have long. We hugged some more, had a cup of tea and then I kissed both Nanny and Granddad goodbye. Mum then took me home. Neither of us said anything, we just held hands. I think we both knew it would only be a matter of a few days. When we got home we had a big cuddle, a cry together, I told my Mum I was so sorry for everything I had done wrong, for the pain I had caused her and I told her how much

I loved her and Dad. She just said, "It's okay." And then we went to bed.

During the night I remember waking up and looking at my watch. I saw the hands move and then stop at 3:30am. I wondered why I had woken up. In the morning, Mum let us sleep in, but when she came to wake us up, I looked at her and I knew Granddad was not with us anymore. I asked her, "When did Granddad die?" She said about 3:30 this morning. I sobbed into my pillow and then felt an immense sense of peace that he had gone to heaven and was no longer in pain, no longer confused, no longer suffering from all the awful hallucinations, and no longer having to take countless tablets every day. He and Nanny used to say if you shook him he'd rattle. Well he wasn't going to rattle anymore, he was going to rest and keep watch over Nanny until her time came. Then they would be together again.

I was 17 at this point and I felt empty. I felt that the whole world had been turned upside down and torn apart. How could he be gone? I felt angry and the pain I felt in my heart was like nothing I had ever felt before. Seeing my nanny crying from her pain, wandering around the home, just sitting in her chair with little giggles escaping followed by a rush of tears and, "I'll be with you soon Boblin," broke my heart in tiny pieces.

They hadn't long celebrated 50 years of marriage together and I remember Nanny had had her hair 'set' especially. They were both dressed up and although Granddad had his best shirt and tie on, he had put his beloved brown chunky knit jumper over the top. Nanny had told him, "Take that bloody thing off!" He just took her by the hand and danced with her. I remember her laughing and calling him, "A daft old sod."

Remembering all of this made me cry so hard, still does today, tears are flowing down my face as I write these words. I miss him so much, so very, very much. I take comfort in the fact he lived to a good age, and he'd lived a happy life with Nanny. I know from the amount of time I spent with Nanny after this that the day Granddad died, she wanted to die too. Her heart broke into thousands of pieces and I believe that when she died a couple of years later, she died of a broken heart. She gave up, and when we were at his funeral and she said, "I'll be with you soon

Boblin." I remember telling her off and running away. Mum told me off and I heard Nanny say, "Leave her, she doesn't understand love yet." I always knew she was a wise woman, my Nanny.

I stayed over at Nanny and Granddad's most nights and at first it felt wrong sleeping where Granddad had, but I knew it was a great comfort to Nanny. I would help her with her medication, clean the home, cook and bake with her and walk with her around the village. She would get cross at me and Aunty Amy who lived next door with Uncle Fred, Granddad's brother, would pop round and tell her off. We would spend hours, the three of us, talking about everything and anything. They would tell me stories of Granddad when he was younger, things they used to get up to together, holidays they had taken when they were first married. It was just what Nanny, and I, needed. I got to know my Nanny and Granddad on a whole new level. I saw how much they had come through together, how deep their love was, how marriage was hard but the saving grace of life. Having a witness for your life and a person to share the difficult times as well as have lots of fun with.

I wanted a marriage that lasted a lifetime and when I would go home I would get out my journals and write down all the advice Nanny and Aunty Amy had given me. What to look for in a man, how to overcome the rows, because there would be plenty of them over the decades. They told me how to be a woman, a wife and a mother. We discussed religion, belief and faith, how they stemmed from a similar thing, but how they were different, how you had to answer to God for everything you did and said, as well as the things you didn't say and do.

Through the endless cups of tea, the long afternoons of talking, baking and walking around the village, I came to realise it wasn't my responsibility to take care of Granddad, even if I wanted to. He was grateful that I helped him look after himself, and this distinction along with many that Nanny and Aunty Amy gave me helped me enormously. It was okay to miss him because I loved him, and Nanny told me, "Love never dies, it just sometimes goes for a walk." She told me to hold onto my memories of him because it makes it easier.

Then I remembered something he had told me when we were on one of our walks, "God brought us to this world and He will take us when He's ready. There's no point fearing death, it comes to us all. If you've lived a good and honest life, you'll go to heaven. If not, then only He knows what He will do with you."

———————

I started reading books on psychology and philosophy as a way of exploring scenarios and theories following Granddad's death. I wasn't studying them as a qualification, my friends were, I was just interested. Philosophy had always interested me since I learnt about Taoism and Buddhism, but now with my granddad dead and my nan's health declining further, revisiting the beliefs in each of these, and exploring Islaam further seemed more important than ever. What would happen to me if I died having not made sense of all these religions? I still couldn't believe that I was a Muslim because it seemed too simple, too easy to just declare your belief to God. I wasn't Catholic so I knew I wouldn't end up in Limbo, but was there somewhere like it for those that had not made up their mind? Did we go to hell or did we go to heaven? Or was it that we stay in the place called 'Hell on Earth' instead of the fiery hell? I mean, come on, let's face it: life on earth can seem like hell at times, especially when there's no forgiveness.

Acceptance of mistakes and forgiveness are things I had never experienced at home. My brother Rob just got moodier and cut me out of his life, until he needed me to take his side in a family fallout, and Ellen just never spoke about anything. She bottled everything up inside and withdrew further into herself. Mum and Dad never liked to talk about problems; everything was just swept under the carpet, pretending as if nothing had happened. I always wanted to discuss things, so of course this was a nuisance. All of this made me grow away from my family and their views more and more over the next couple of years.

Nanny was still with us, albeit very weak. Mum needed help taking care of her, and her medical needs were getting too much for Mum to cope with. Nanny needed to be nursed properly and it was decided she should go into a home. I hated the idea. We should look after her. Why send her away when she needed the ones she loved most in the world around her? How could we leave her alone with complete strangers? I could stay with her like I had been doing. It was wrong. I was angry. I was powerless to stop it. I was at college and I was a bad girl. I took drugs so obviously had no idea of what was right and wrong, and I was a huge disappointment so I had no say in the matter whatsoever.

I felt like I was losing control and nothing in my world was making sense anymore. I remember going to see Aunty Amy again and her saying to me that no matter what happens, I should always believe. She never said what to believe in, but she told me my faith was my faith and I had to figure out what it meant to me. So, I started thinking about who I was, what I knew, and over the next few years I started to understand what Aunty Amy and Nanny had told me shortly after Granddad had died, "Religion, faith, and belief are all different. They come from the same place, inside of you, but they are different, for you and for everyone. No one can take it away from you, only God. You leave it up to Him and trust in Him and you'll be alright."

---

1. Except when I looked in the mirror and saw my mother looking back at me, talk about bringing you back down to earth with a bang!
2. A trip was the "journey" we took when on acid. As our visual cortex was stimulated in a way other drugs rarely did, we saw things that weren't there, or things that were, but in a completely new way. We also explored our inner space, acid is a drug like no other, it literally opened up new pathways in your brain.
3. Horse racing :)
4. Under the influence of MDMA, practically everyone was your friend and you loved everything. I read once that there was a sharp decrease in football hooliganism when Es first came on the scene. That's the love power of the E. It doesn't last forever, of course.
5. A mixed drink made of liquor and water with sugar and spices and served hot.

SEVEN

MEETING RAMO

College was nearly over, exams were being taken and it was time for some major summer parties. Helter Skelter's big summer blowout was the party everyone was talking about. I was in the common room at college when I first saw the flyer. I didn't know why, but I had this *very* strong urge and desire to go. I asked so many people if they were going and if I could get a lift with them. Unfortunately everyone's car was full, as was the case with most Helter Skelters or Dreamscapes[1]. There was a girl called Lynn who wanted to go and she said if she could get a ticket, then of course she would take me. I told her if you take me, I'll buy your ticket. She was pleased with the offer and then said she wouldn't go unless her boyfriend Neil could go. So like a fool I offered to buy his ticket too. Things were set. I was going. It was all I could think about. I had to be there.

About a week before, I stupidly gave Lynn the tickets for her and Neil and arranged a meet up point. She took the tickets off me and told me she would speak with Neil that night and call me back to finalise the meeting point. She never got back to me; so that was £50 down the drain and now no way of getting to Helter Skelter. By this time I was working in a pub in Peterborough and I had got to know the guy who owned the record shop just around the corner, so I went to see him. He managed to get me a lift with a group of people I didn't know. I got there and it felt amazing. I was in a rave of more than ten thousand people all by myself. I loved it! I could go where I wanted, when I wanted without meeting up with people at a certain time or place. I went on the fairground rides that were all part of the Helter Skelter experience, had hot cups of tea, chatted to people and had a blast. Then that urge to be somewhere at a certain time came back. All I could think of was getting to the techno room in time for DJ Loftgroover, who I got to know later on as Tony; a really nice guy. His music was amazing[2]. Whilst most people tried to dance to the beat, I was more interested in the mental journey that overlaid the beat. I have no idea what it is called, but I called it the 'off beat'. A mutual friend of ours Steve, also known as HMS, may he rest in peace, also played the same kind of music and I loved it!!

Saturday 6th July came around and the year was 1996. I was in the Techno Room with its bouncy floor. You could just stand there and you would move up and down. The energy levels and the vibes that night were amazing and all I kept thinking was, *this is wicked!*[3] It was only after I had finished dancing to Tony's set that I looked over my right shoulder and saw ramO. I felt as though I had been hit by a lorry. He was talking to this girl called Nikki. I knew she was a friend of Sara's, my friend Tammy's friend. I went over to ask her if Tammy and Sara were there, knowing full well neither of them was, just so I could strike up a conversation with the guy she was talking to. I asked what his name was and before long we were bantering with each other. I liked this guy, a lot. He made me laugh, he made me think, he loved techno and he was the sexiest thing on two legs I had ever seen. I knew he was going to be mine. We spent the rest of the night together, dancing, laughing and generally taking the piss out of each other. We did our fair share of kissing too. I tingled every time he touched me, and it was like he sent electricity through my body every time he held my face in his hands and kissed me gently, and passionately, on the lips. I loved being in his company, he was like no one else I had ever met before. When the morning came, I gave him my number and he said he would call me Tuesday at 7pm. I have no idea how I got home that morning, but I do remember sitting by the phone on Tuesday night from 6:30pm waiting for the phone to ring. When it did, at 7pm precisely, I let it ring a few times. It is the only time he has ever been on time for anything.

After that initial phone call we spoke a lot more on the phone. He would drive all the way from Banbury in Oxfordshire, where he was working as a video game developer on the official Atlanta '96 Olympics game. Living just outside of Banbury and travelling to collect me from Friday Bridge in Cambridgeshire, or Peterborough if I was working, was a big deal to me. I didn't know anyone else who would do that. He took me to my first Diehard which was in Leicester, and this is where I found many of the friends that still surround me today. They are the ones that became my new family; my Diehard family. When I met the Diehard techno heads, not only did I meet a group of crazy party people, but I met a group of people who held down a job, some were doing degrees, and some had their own businesses. They had an interest in all kinds of subjects, crazy ideas and they were up for a mission anywhere any time. The techno room was where my friendship with Jay 'the cream of Manchester' started, along with friendships with Anthea, Mazzy Maz, Grizzwald, Brendan, Sally, Paul, Karl, Mel, Cassie, Lee, Roxanne, Alan and Jess, and many more.

The people ramO knew were my kind of people. I wasn't strange for wanting to talk about deep stuff, or a nerd for wanting a better life. I wasn't 'up myself' for wanting to run my own business. I was just another person on her own mission. My faith in people was restored. Life was good again. Very good.

The reason why it was so good was because Diehard brought together a whole lot of people from across the country, of different professions, different socio-economic groups; and it was the only place where they didn't sell alcohol. This made Diehard special. It didn't attract the beer- monsters; it didn't attract those spoiling for a fight. It was PEACE LOVE AND UNITY at its very best. People didn't judge others, or if they did, they kept it to themselves, and everyone knew everyone else; if they didn't, then they would do by the end of the night. It didn't matter which DJs were playing, they were all 'bang on', if it was Friday night, we were off to Leicester, we were off to Diehard. We'd leave home when everyone else was coming in from the pubs and we would go home when everyone was waking up. Diehard pills were the best in the country and so was the amphetamine. It wasn't billy I was taking any more, it was bass. It wasn't cut with anything and you needed a much smaller amount.

It was safer and the buzz was even better. The Diehard car park was also part of the experience. We would spend at least an hour, possibly two or three there afterwards talking, listening to tunes loudly and discussing where to go next. Which part of the country were we going to: Coventry? Banbury? Sheffield? Milton Keynes? Wales even. Anywhere was possible, and anything was possible. They were some of the most exciting times of my life, and I loved every moment of the Diehard days.

In Diehard, being given water that was spiked with drugs was never an option; it was just not the done thing. Sometimes when others poured water over their own heads because of being so hot from dancing, and you looked at them and smiled, you could guarantee they'd give you their water and tell you to pour it over your own head, if they hadn't done it for you. We were in sync with each other. We were the Diehard family and I was becoming known as ramO's Mrs. Never Dawn, but by this time I had fallen hook, line and sinker for this man they called ramO, the techno terrorist.

ramO was full on with everything. He wore a balaclava rolled up as a beanie hat, pulling it down for effect when the music became particularly banging. He wore it even inside the hottest of raves, took piss-taking to an extreme and would argue black was blue if he wanted to, most of the time just to get you to agree with his point of view or to get you to see another person's point of view. He loved his techno hard and fast. He wanted to party all weekend. I had never laughed, debated or partied so hard in my life, but strangely enough, I was more careful now about what I did and which parties we went to afterwards.

Since I started seeing ramO, my life was beginning to make more sense. Our conversations were deep. We talked about the future, we talked about religion and philosophy, ideas, ethics, morals, and we talked about absolutely everything. We didn't agree on everything, and to this day we never have, but that is what made being with ramO so special. It didn't matter if I agreed with him, because it was more about the discussion, the viewpoints and the challenge of understanding something much bigger than ourselves. ramO was sorting my head out, and it was a good job too because someone had to. My life needed to get back on track because hanging out with some of the people I had been hanging out with, my life was taking a path I didn't want it to. Before meeting ramO, the amount of drugs I was taking had seen me go down a slippery slope. It was time to sort myself out, and ramO was just what I needed.

My mum was happier too. She could see a huge improvement in me. She was more relaxed around me and for the first time in a very long time we were laughing together. ramO had taught me to respect my mum and dad, even though I thought I had been. If I was ever rude to my parents in front of him, he would 'have a word' with me about how it is not right to be rude to your parents. I began to realise that over the years I had become so caught up in my own self-hatred and had blamed my Mum for so much that I had forgotten about all the good things both her and dad had done for Rob, Ellen and me. I had forgotten about all the fun times we'd had on family holidays at Kelling Heath, in Devon and Cornwall. I had forgotten about the fact that they both worked really hard to give us everything they could, even if the three of us were too ungrateful to realise it. ramO gave me a new way of seeing my mum and dad, and the more he helped me see who I was, the more I fell in love with him.

The more we spoke the more I learnt about Islaam, because as it happens he was a Muslim, and he was of Palestinian heritage. I had so many questions for him, I wanted to know everything about Islaam, I wanted to know if he had ever been to Palestine and when we planned on going. This was the first time I learnt about the Palestine/Israel conflict, and before he could tell me much more about it, I stopped him. I didn't want any family baggage clouding my judgement on the situation. He was deeply connected to the issue and I wanted an unbiased opinion about the whole situation. The the more I found out about it all – the involvement of Britain, the UN, and the continued support of the Christian and Jewish communities in the USA and beyond – the more I stood by the Palestinians.

The more I learned about what it meant to be a Muslim, the more I knew I was one. All those doubts I'd had in my head, but never in my heart, disappeared. I realised that the moment I had completed the project for Miss Eddon back in religious education classes when I was 15, and had that feeling of weightlessness and inner peace on the school trip where I had felt faint and felt as though I wanted to cry, more of relief than sadness, that was the moment my body knew I was going to be a

Muslim. My head and it's never ending questions and need for reasoning just had to catch up.

Shortly after ramO and I had been seeing each other, we went to see my Nanny in the nursing home where she was living. It had been a few weeks since I had seen her as I had been working hard in Peterborough. When we walked in Nanny was smiling, and wearing her favourite blue jumper and her navy slacks.

She asked who my handsome chap was and I told her his name was ramO.

"Rambo? Did you say Rambo?"

"No Nanny, he's called ramO," I said giggling.

"Ah. Rambo, that's a funny name. Hahaha! You young 'uns today."

Nanny had lost lots of weight and was getting tired much quicker. I knew she didn't have long to go but this time I wasn't sad. I knew she wanted to go. I knew she wanted to go and be with Granddad and now I had ramO, I understood why. In the short time I had known ramO, I had begun to picture my future and, for the first time ever, I saw myself as an elderly lady like Nanny, sitting beside him, watching our grandchildren together. Nanny knew it too and told me I had a special one and I had best keep hold of him. I promised her I would and she reminded me it would be hard, but if it wasn't hard, it wasn't worth having.

Even in her last days of forgetting things two minutes after she had said something or we had told her something, she still knew the most important things to say. She was wise until her dying day; which wasn't long after we visited her.

I went to see her in the Chapel of Rest with Dad, and whilst he was at Granddad's grave, I went into the chapel and held her hand. I kissed her on the forehead and then again on the cheek. She'd had her hair done again and it brought back memories of her golden wedding anniversary to Granddad. I kissed her again and told her Granddad was waiting for her, and how much he had missed her. I told her all the things I had wanted to say, apologised for all the things I wanted to apologise for, knowing she would call me a 'silly wench' for apologising to her. I cried but not for her because I knew she was at peace, no longer going to rattle if you shook her due to the amount of tablets she'd been taking, but because I was going to miss her. I cried because I knew I would never hear her laugh again, never taste her treacle tarts again and then I realised these were all selfish reasons. What was best for her was for God to take her to be with Him, and Granddad now. For Him do we come from and to Him we do return. Never be afraid of dying, it is the only thing we can guarantee in this life as my granddad had told me many years earlier.

ramO helped me through the loss of my Nanny and came to the funeral with me. It felt so good to have him by my side holding my hand. A few months later, my friend Jaime called me to tell me that Brian, a mutual friend, had died. I needed to get out, I needed to go somewhere for a joint. I needed to be alone with ramO. I needed to just be.

Losing Brian at such a young age made me realise that if I was going to live on this earth, I was going to grab every opportunity that inspired me and felt right. I was not going to get to the age of 50 saying I wish I had done this or that. I was going to grab life with both hands and party like it was 1999. Good old Prince, Symbol, 'The Artist Formerly Known As Prince', or whatever he wanted to call himself! Whatever his name is or was, that tune was my tune of the moment. I came up with two new life mottos: 'Laugh to live and live to laugh' and 'Love your life, it's the only one you've got, and if you don't love it, change it'.

ramO and I continued raving every weekend. We hosted many after parties at what had become our home in Banbury. Grizzwald came to live with us and I got to know Chris, the person behind the long hair and goofy behaviour. He wasn't just a party head to me anymore, he was like my younger brother, a pain in the backside and yet a friend. ramO and I continued enjoying many deep conversations about religion, faith and belief at our own little after party, after everyone had left to go home or Chris had gone on a mad mission somewhere. Some of the questions I asked ramO were not things he had considered before. Some of the things I had learnt turned out to be more cultural than Islaamic.

With the depth of conversations going to whole new levels whilst we took acid, and the different thought processes being 'opened' due to the new neuro-pathways our brains were using, gave us a really strong connection with our faith, our friendship and what would turn out to be the strongest relationship next to God, either of us would ever have again. Not only did taking drugs and meeting ramO open my mind further than I could ever have imagined, it blew my mind to pieces, quite literally some would say.

I know if he had asked me to marry him just two months after having met him, I would have said yes. Instead, I had to wait 18 months for him to ask, six months after we bought our first home together in Oxford; I was 19 years old, holding down a sales job to get the training I needed to run my own business – just like I had been advised to do two years earlier by the many business men and women in Eastbourne – I was engaged to be married, and I owned my own home. My life was coming together and I was beginning to realise I had to follow my gut instinct. It had led me to talk to the 'foreigners' in the village, it had made me want to go to Mecca, to go on Hajj, it had led me down the path of working in hotels across the country, it had led me to Helter Skelter and little did I know, it would save me a lot of lost money due to dodgy business clients in the future.

---

1. These were two of the bigger regular events, one every three months or so, thousands of people went, multiple rooms each with a different type of dance music, and usually with an outdoor area with a fun fair. Going on the rides while you're on drugs, gives the fun an extra dimension lol
2. Some called it Hard Techno, some called it Gabber, and some called it Speed Core. It was hard, fast, and "banging". Perfect music for billy.
3. That's the good wicked not the bad wicked I'll have you know. Like Michael Jackson's cool type of "bad" instead of the simply bad "bad"!

EIGHT
OXFORD LIFE

With its romantic spires and historical buildings, libraries and museums, theatres and galleries, I was able to lose myself in a world I once thought only existed on TV. I was able to visit all the places that I had heard about whilst watching TV or reading books. I was able to shop in the Covered Market for my deli items followed by a nice relaxing coffee in the bounty of cafes and coffee shops. I was free to read a book and not have someone stare at or criticise me for being strange, in fact it was the first time in my life I would be interrupted from my book by someone who had either read the book I was reading, wanted to read it or was simply interested in what the book was about. It was a city where my love of books was shared and encouraged, and the variety of books I read grew to genres I had never considered before.

I loved living and working in Oxford. I would spend hours in the bookshops and cafes, walking around the city just taking it all in. My life was already more than I had dreamed it would ever be, and a far cry from Friday Bridge, Wisbech and Peterborough! Life was confusing and yet simple. I was in love, yet still didn't love myself. I was working towards a dream of having my own business, but still not clear how it was actually going to happen. I was a Muslim but my lifestyle was far from Islaamic. I loved food so why was I still purging? I was an honest and straightforward person, so why was I being so deceitful to so many people? I was hiding the drugs and the purging from so many people; so many people thought I had it all together, so why did I feel like I was falling apart? Others thought I was confident yet, inside, I was so insecure. My way of getting around it was to talk. I kept remembering one of the speakers at one of the business events in the Eastbourne Hotel, "Act like you are and you will become." If I act like I am confident, then one day I will be confident.

If I act like I am successful, then one day I will be successful.

If I act like a Muslim, then one day I will be a Muslim; and it was this last one that had my head in a spin. I already was a Muslim, so why did I have to act like it? And if I was already a Muslim, then surely when I talked, made people laugh, achieved great things at work, then I was already confident and successful? So why was I not feeling it? What was it that was preventing me from seeing what others saw in me? Was this a veil that God had put over my eyes to prevent me from being arrogant and egotistical? I hoped so because if there was one thing that I never wanted to be was arrogant, because I had seen what arrogance looked like when I was working in the hotels and restaurants. People thought that just because I was a waitress or barmaid, they could speak *at* me with no regard. I was nothing to them because I was *their server* but as Bob Hoskins says in the film *Maid in Manhattan*, "It takes dignity to serve people, and although we may serve them, we are not their servants."

I never wanted to make people feel inferior to me because it is rude to do so and everyone is equal, as it says in the Qur'aan; and it was the equality element of the Hajj that had made me want to go. Everyone in the white robes, without indication of money, intellect, status, all worshipping God and making the Pilgrimage that the final Prophet made. Everyone equal in the eyes of God, so now all I had to do was believe I was equal, believe I deserved the love ramO gave me, believe I could achieve anything I wanted to and believe that I am liked by all the people that said they liked me.

Our life in Oxford was pretty hectic. We worked really hard during the week, ramO travelling nearly 100 miles a day by car, or flying 500 to 1000 miles a week for his software consultancy roles all over Europe. With all his travelling and my sheer determination to learn and do as much as possible, we were keen to let off steam when the weekend came. We would party all night Friday night and all night Saturday night, and if it was a Bank Holiday, it was time for a Bank Holiday bender; May was a pretty messy month! We travelled 500 miles on average each weekend, sometimes we'd go 1000 miles to party in Scotland and Wales. We partied in Amsterdam and Rotterdam and we loved it! Our regular weekends involved us travelling to Leicester, then to Coventry to be with Russell, Ciaran, 'Mad' John, Greg AKA Jesus, and Alex AKA Bluey AKA 'male Alex'. From Coventry to Milton Keynes then back to Oxford, and many times there were other cities or towns thrown in for a quick chill out. Saturday's in Coventry with Russell and the gang were some of the best Saturday's of my life. We continued to party and talk rubbish on every subject known to man. We would often forget what we were talking about, let cups of tea go cold and joints go out. But the joints would not go out for long.

Lighters would go missing and I would always get the blame for some reason, maybe because my combats and fleece had loads of pockets and when emptied at least three lighters would be found. "It wasn't done on purpose I promise, it just happened." Pockets are great things, combats are even better. They were my raving essentials along with my Adidas trainers, a black vest top, a hair band and a bottle of water.

I came up with an acronym for Adidas which I still smile at today: After Dancing I Deserve A Spliff. There was another acronym for FILA that I liked but as I was loyal to the Adidas three stripe, like thousands of other ravers, I would never wear the brand. I still to this day only wear Adidas, apart from one pair of Saucony running trainers. I am one of Adidas' true fans in both the marketing term and the everyday people's term. Adidas all the way, especially now Stella McCartney has been designing for them! Nice!

At least one weekend a month we would head to Wales on the Saturday morning after Diehard or Deathrow Techno in Bristol to spend with Nic, Jan and Alexs AKA 'female Alexs or Welsh Alexs'. They along with Russell, Ciaran, 'Mad' John, Greg AKA Jesus, and Alex were the chosen few ramO and I would spend our time with. Out of all our raving friends I loved them the most. We spent many fun and crazy times together in many different mental states. They knew ramO and I were both Muslim and religion came up a few times but it was never an issue.

One of the biggest hurdles I have always faced is believing that people actually like me. I remember after one of our first house parties in our new home, it finally dawned on me that people had actually stopped calling me "ramO's Mrs" and had actually started calling me Dawn. ramO's friends were now my friends, and there were many that I really liked. I loved the way Pete, Jill and Rich took the piss out of each other; and I will always remember Jill telling me if she didn't take the piss out of me, she didn't like me so I had better get used to it.

Then there was Si, or rather Shiny Si. He was, and still is, a really funny guy who just captures you under his spell. He would annoy the hell out of me in a club because just as I was peaking[1] or getting into the guts of a set he would come and tap me on the shoulder and start talking to me. NOOOO!!! I want to dance!! He would proceed to tell me that such and such a DJ had played this tune at such and such a club on such and such a weekend. Honestly, if you wanted to know anything about the DJ sets played in many of the clubs we went to, then Si is the 'raving rainman' with a great big heart. Si still has a big chunk of my heart somewhere in Middlesbrough with him. He always will have.

Then there was Craig and Michelle, both from Middlesbrough and although the banter was equally as funny, it wasn't as harsh as Pete, Jill and Rich's. Craig was one of the funniest people I had ever met, and I am sure if he and ramO ever had the opportunity for a comedy sketch, they would have a huge following. I can remember crying with laughter even when I wasn't on drugs, which was becoming less of an occurrence now. He still makes me laugh to this day when we speak or meet up, especially with his undying faith that one day Middlesbrough will win the FA Cup[2]. Michelle was the encyclopaedia Britannica when it came to 70s music and after eight, mad hours of techno, we would all chill out together and if we were chilling out in her home, it meant some 70s tunes. I loved and admired the love she had for something no one else in our group had. She liked it and that was all that mattered. She taught me a lot about myself, and about the 70s! She was one of those friends that I knew would stand the test of time and 15 years on, she is still a really good friend of mine.

There were others we met across the country who became great friends, such as Rolf. He is one of the kindest people I have ever met and would always stop by when he was passing the A34 on his way back to Bristol after one of his long drives dealing with high-end printers.

These friends, along with the guys and girls from Wales and Coventry, are the ones who got to *see* me. They were the ones that helped me realise they liked me for me, not just because I was ramO's girlfriend. I was likeable and fun to be around, even if I did get on my soap box every now and then. They accepted me and it felt good to be accepted by someone other than the man I was waiting to propose to me.

When ramO did finally propose, they were the first ones we told about our plans to get married. Jan, Nick, and Alex (Bluey) came with us to Egypt when we got married, with Nic failing to impress my mother-in-law by forgetting his shoes. ramO and I thought it was hilarious and such a 'Nic' thing to do, but not the best way to be remembered by the mother-in-law!

Life on the friendship front was good, now everything else just had to work out.

One day I decided to visit as many recruitment agencies as possible. I was on a mission. I wanted to gain as much business experience as possible and one day whilst I was registering with a recruitment agency, I met a lady called Jenny. She was probably the most helpful and honest recruitment agent I have ever met, both as an employee and employer – she actually read the CV and job descriptions properly! She advised me on a plan of action, placed me in a variety of roles that would give me the vast experience in all the departments I would need as a business owner and in part it was thanks to her that within the next two years, I left the life of an employee and started my own business with ramO.

During those two years I worked in an accounting department for a large national building firm as a data entry clerk, then as a sales administrator for a national telecoms company. I worked as a secretary and PA to a Senior Project Manager for an International Building firm, organising the build of one of Oxford's newest hospitals. I worked for one of Europe's largest IT peripherals companies, a local newspaper, an insurance firm, one of Europe's largest business and public data handling firms selling and analysing business and consumer information, a software development company and a media consultancy. Two of those positions, including the media consultancy were both permanent positions, although I was made redundant from both because of short-sighted management and an oversight in financials. Being made redundant from both was more of a blessing than a hindrance though and benefitted me greatly. As a permanent employee, they spent time training me, something I vowed to always do with my future employees. Having been placed in a variety of roles, I learnt so much about business processes, strategy development and management; and of course the dreaded office politics, something I was very keen to see the back of when I started my own company.

The one thing I couldn't, and didn't, want to deal with was the people who worked for these firms moaning from the day I walked in to the day I left. I would always ask, "If you hate your job so much, why are you still here?"

Answers were always, "There are no jobs out there," "I can't afford to leave my job," or, "I haven't found a job I like yet." I just couldn't believe what I was hearing! Here I was living in Oxford with loads of bookshops, training centres, colleges and universities, not to mention pages upon pages of jobs being listed every week in the local and regional press and these people couldn't find a job! Many of them said they couldn't afford to retrain as something else but just listening to them and the amount they spent on booze, clothes or cigarettes, in just six months they could pay for many of the training courses being offered across the city (many of them free).

One person I worked with replaced her whole entire wardrobe every season to keep up with the latest fashions and yet moaned she could not afford to do the degree she wanted to do.

Er, excuse me… how about keeping your entire wardrobe for the year? Stop buying stupidly expensive shoes, spending a fortune on wine and champagne every weekend and invest in your mind and your future? Maybe you wouldn't have to fix the outside so much if you spent a little time fixing the inside!

It seemed crazy to me and yet here I was still taking drugs, which had started as a way to numb the pain I was feeling aged 15, and was now just a way of staying awake to dance during the mad weekend sessions. They were also a way explore the different possibilities of the mind and discuss the many philosophical arguments with ramO – who, if anything – is a great philosopher and will argue black is blue all night, sometimes to get to the base point of an idea and other times just to be a pain in the backside. Either way, it provided many amusing ideas and reasonings.

But this, I had realised, had to come to an end if I was going to live my life by God's word, as described in the Qur'aan. The parties were reducing in frequency and length because Diehard had been busted, Helter Skelter was not as great as it had once been and we had found a new place to party: North at The Void, in Hanley, Stoke – Friday night was North and it finished at 2am which meant we could head off to Wales sooner and spend a great weekend with Jan, Nic and Alexs.

I had to fix inside my head and heal my heart properly, even though by now, the only issues I felt I had were the family problems and my fighting the 'urge to purge'. ramO, Jan, Nic and Alexs helped me to do this in the beautiful setting of the country of Wales. We watched films together, ate together, partied together and spent time in the hills together. Just being together was enough.

Talking with Jan about her losing her mum made me stop and think about my own relationship with my mum. My mum was alive and I wanted to stop the negative patterns of behaviour we had between us. I was lucky my mum was still alive. I had a chance to make it better.

Being at Jan and Nic's was great because Jan and I would cook together, we'd all eat together and this helped to stop the 'urge' but I also couldn't get away with it in Jan and Nic's house. Their bathroom was downstairs. They would have heard me, even though I had gotten quite good at not making much noise when purging.

It had also begun to make me feel immensely guilty. ramO and I had been on holidays overseas to Bulgaria and I had seen my first 'serious' beggars, people that needed to beg because the country didn't provide housing or 'Big Issue' type initiatives for people to get off the street. These people were hungry and here I was throwing up a beautiful meal just because of an insecurity that had started back in high school. I no longer needed to be thin, but the memories of being teased, the image of the BMI chart in the doctor's surgery that had clearly defined me as 'obese' due to my height to weight ratio, even though I was fit and healthy and it was more due to muscle than fat, the pattern that had emerged from eating and purging had created an instinctive reaction in my brain. When you eat, you purge. Fighting that after a meal was hard, especially when it was a Sunday Lunch with dessert. My stomach felt full and it was painful. Sometimes I had to lie down on the bed upstairs but Jan or Alexs would soon come upstairs to me to see if I was alright; and with their help, their friendship, travelling overseas and the love of a good man, I was becoming alright.

I still purged a couple of times a week, down from seven or eight times a week, but this was progress in the right direction.

We'd been in Oxford for about two years when I discovered this little white door that when opened would lead you into a world of literature spanning hundreds of years. I have no recollection what the shop was called, in fact I do not think I knew what it was called back then, but oh… it was heaven! There were books in this little piece of literacy heaven that were so delicate I remember getting such butterflies at the thought of standing so close to them! The smell of the books was one of the most mesmerising smells I have ever had the pleasure to smell and the whole place was a little rabbit warren filled with book shelves, floor to ceiling book shelves. The man in the shop smiled at me and even though a word never passed either of our lips we both knew we felt the same about books. He just left me in my daze of happiness, completely spell bound. When I left, wide-eyed and filled with happiness, he said his only words to me with a grin on his face, "Come again if only to breathe it all in even deeper."

I replied, "I would love to! Thank you."

I drifted to my next stop, The Oxford Islaamic Centre on the corner of Cornmarket and George Street. I remember walking in blissfully happy, smiling away to myself and asking if they provided Arabic and Islaamic courses. They were not able to help me then in the way I had wanted, but what they did do was hand me a beautiful copy of The Holy Qur'aan. Now this was no ordinary copy. This was a beautiful edition with the thinnest pages I had ever seen, a beautiful blue hard back copy with gold leaf on the edge of the pages. When I asked how much it cost the man inside told me it was a gift. I remember feeling that light headed feeling I had experienced when I was on the school trip with Miss Eddon learning about the Hajj. I asked the gentleman if he was sure I could have it as a gift and he told me, "Of course, it is our pleasure."

I cannot remember the drive home; all I remember is wrapping the Qur'aan up in my coat and placing it very carefully on the front seat next to me. I couldn't stop placing my hand on it, whenever driving allowed, and when I got home I remember dumping everything in the armchair and sitting on the couch cross legged staring at the cover. I had here, in front of me, my very own Qur'aan; what a beautiful copy it was!

I still treasure it today. It is the edition I will leave to my grandchildren and future generations of my family. And be warned boys, if you damage it in any way, or do not teach your children how to take care of it, I will haunt you forever!

ramO came home that night about 7:30pm and I had not even prepared dinner. I was still sat on the couch stroking the pages and the cover. I told him about everything that had happened that day and how magical it had been. He just smiled at me, gave me a hug and we ordered Chinese takeout. I didn't purge that night.

Shortly after being given my first Qur'aan, I came across a two-volume set of books called *The Choice* by Ahmed Deedat, a very well respected scholar on Christian/Muslim dialogue. I then found more books and it was as though being given this Qur'aan had opened up the floodgates of books on Islaam, and good ones at that.

I was challenged on many levels. I realised that the way we were partying and taking drugs, my bulimic purging and wine drinking all had to be revised. My life had to change. I needed to step up and be counted. I had to focus on what I wanted not just for this life, but for the next life. My life was not just about living in the present; it was about my future on this earth, my children's future and my future after I have left this earth.

It made me start thinking about my family and my duty to them, not just as a daughter, but as a Muslim daughter, and how God will judge me for the way I have behaved, the way in which I have spoken to them and whether or not I have respected them or not. Being confronted with my Islaamic duties made me realise many things about my behaviour; I had to call my mum and dad, my sister and my brother. I had to make amends for the mistakes I had made and put things right.

It didn't turn out very well. Rob, my brother, who had tried to stab me in my home in Banbury after I offered him a cup of tea, thinking it had been spiked with drugs, and had only been prevented from doing so by two of his friends Mark and Peter, didn't want anything to do with me. Ellen, who was now married to her husband Paul, didn't say much and although I wasn't aware at the time, wasn't having a very good time of it either. My mum didn't want to go over old ground and 'keep dragging up the past' and didn't feel we needed to improve anything. Dad was same old Dad, head in his fishing magazines or by the river bank. And so I just had to write to my father and get things sorted with him.

So my best efforts to make amends had either failed or were on the road to somewhere, only God knew where. I focused on the other areas of my life that I could make a difference with.

I focused on work, planned my wedding to ramO, made a promise to myself on a monthly basis I would not purge and started to reduce my drug- taking even more. North was only a two o'clocker[3] so I didn't really need to take chemicals anymore. Smoking joints I did not consider as drug- taking any more than cigarette smokers consider themselves drug-takers. When you had a cup of tea or were stressed out, you made a spliff. And I had become a spliff-making connoisseur by this point following a spliff rolling lesson after Diehard with Karl several years earlier. And as Karl had said, "If you are going to smoke a spliff, at least smoke a decent one!" I agreed it wasn't just the smoking of the spliff that was important, it was the art of rolling one that should also be enjoyed. I perfected my art, just as I was trying to perfect all the other 'not so perfect' areas of my life.

Through all the books I had found in Oxford, I discovered if I wanted to go on Hajj, I needed a Declaration of Faith certificate, I guess to prove to the Saudis that I was a Muslim and not someone who was going to blow up the Ka3ba! This can only be obtained by saying the declaration in a mosque or in front of an Islaamic official.

ramO and I were off to get married in Egypt so why not make this declaration of faith, which I had said to myself all those years ago, legal in Egypt? I couldn't think of a reason not to, and we managed to get an appointment with an Imaam at Al-Azhar mosque in the heart of Cairo just a few days before we were married. It wouldn't interfere with the wedding my mother-in-law to-be had organised or the couple of days we had booked in Sharm El-Sheikh − at Hotel Cannabesh, which seemed funny and appropriate for us at the time − so we went ahead and did it.

My mother-in-law pointed out to me that my current wardrobe of clothes was not really appropriate to go and take my declaration in so she lent me one of her blouses. Slightly too big and with 'power' shoulders − not my taste at all − but it did the job.

When we walked into the mosque I was awestruck at the beauty of it all. The artwork, the calligraphy, and the staircase, everything was beautiful. Whilst we were in the office of the Imaam, everything was going well. I had given my personal details in English and ramO and his mum translated it into Arabic. I said the declaration and then the Imaam asked me what my Muslim name was. Having not realised I needed one; I looked at ramO confused and lost.

What was wrong with my name? Where did it say in the Qur'aan I needed a Muslim name? Surely the Muslim names were the names of the people who were Muslim? Did he mean an Arabic name? And if so why would I want an Arabic name if I am English?

I started to panic and then my mother-in-law suggested to satisfy the Imaam, to avoid a scene and get the job done, we should just go with the Arabic translation of my name: Fajr, as in sunrise, also the name of the morning prayer.

I had not, until this point, realised what a perfect name my mother had given me. It resonated with me on so many levels. Dawn: a new beginning, the name of the morning prayer, the first rays of sunshine; and in those moments sat in front of the Imaam, I loved my mum more than I had ever remembered loving her before.

It wasn't until we arrived back at the apartment and had a cup of tea that my head started spinning. I had felt so happy and peaceful, and had almost floated back to the apartment. But having that cup of tea and sitting down made me take stock of what I had just done. I had signed a legal document without my mum being there. I had made a choice about my life which would make her so unhappy, so scared, and unlike the drugs which I had enjoyed most weekends over the years, which were illegal, this was legal! Printed and signed in black and white. Other than buying a house or a car, I had made the first biggest real legal life choice without my mum being present, in a foreign country, and it was a rejection of many of the things that she had wanted for me. I cried my eyes out.

I sobbed for about half an hour. ramO lay with me on the couch just holding me and stroking my hair. He wiped the tears from my eyes and told me everything was going to be alright. I remember it as if it was yesterday. I wasn't scared about anything, I felt so peaceful and happy. The only thing that was worrying me was the fact that my mother was going to be angry with me. She's my mum; the one that raised me, the one that gave birth to me; and here I was rejecting her and the life she had given me. This was a big thing, because I had finally done something for me, something for my own future happiness and I had not thought about anyone else's reaction or input in this choice at all. I had confirmed that the answers I had been looking for all this time, I was satisfied with. The religion of Islaam was the answer to my questions. I had not asked permission to do this. This was something I had wanted, and had been, for six years.

So why did it feel so different now I had a legal document; a piece of paper; a certificate for something I had been learning about? Is this how it feels to graduate from University after years of study? Or was it something much deeper, more profound? Was I just focusing on the fact my mum would be cross with me just as a way of dealing with the enormity of the situation? I didn't know then, and I don't know now, all I knew then was this is now legal and I need another cup of tea.

My mum arrived in Cairo, with my sister and my father, the day after I made my declaration. My dad and brother had both decided not come for whatever reason and I had to accept that. It was awful not having my dad there at my wedding and I felt as though there was a big void at the side of my mum where he should have been. That was his place, beside my mum and had been for the last 20 years. Why was he not there? He broke my heart by not being there.

My brother not being there was also hard but after our 'encounter' in Banbury a couple of years earlier, it was somewhat of a relief; but it still didn't seem right not to have my brother at my wedding, he is my brother. He should have been there, but he chose not to and it felt as though the knife he had tried to stab me with before had gone through me.

My family was broken and I wondered how much of it was my fault. Where could I take responsibility for my actions, because the more I learnt about Islaam the more I realised that I am responsible for everything I say and do and will be accountable for it all on the Day of Judgement. Unlike Christianity, Muslims didn't believe Jesus died for our sins; and unlike some of the Christians I knew, I wasn't going to leave a trail of upset behind me as I went. I made my decision to be accountable for everything I did from then on.

———————————————

1. Feeling the full effect of the drugs.
2. Craig and Si – it's not going to happen, sorry dudes!!
3. It shut at 2am.

NINE

GETTING DOWN TO BUSINESS

One of the ways I chose to be accountable for my life was to take responsibility for my own future. I could not shake the idea of running a business from my mind and the opportunity came about when the firm I had started working for in 1999 decided to make nine people redundant, some of us had only been taken on nine months before. I will admit I was really upset. I had just bought a Peugeot 309 automatic with electric everything. It was black and I was in love with it. To this day, of all the cars I have had, that has been my favourite car. Driving along the A34 all windows open, sunroof open, tunes on loud (just so I could hear over the sound of the wind!) either singing along at the top of my voice or tapping and bouncing along. I caused a few heads to turn and made a few people laugh and smile as I drove along but I didn't care, I love singing and I love dancing, if I can do it whilst driving then so be it. I am a careful driver, having lost a friend at the age of 11 to a drunk driver, a school friend in a road accident when I was 14 and two friends several months earlier in 1999, I took it easy on the road. I have learnt through the loss of my friends and my attempted suicide when I was 14 to treasure life. It is a gift and through Islaam I was learning that it is not our duty to take a life, our own or someone else's. To kill one person is as if you have killed the whole of humanity and to save a life is as if you have saved the whole of humanity.

Being made redundant was however the biggest blessing, something I was about to realise as ramO, Alex, Jill, Pete, two other friends and I flew off to the Gran Canaries for a holiday. Two weeks in the sun to swim, party and think. It was great. We went to a few clubs, lounged around on the beach, I danced in the sea to the tunes playing in my head and we all had a great time. There were some moments when the heat between us rose, but when you have four fiery characters in the mix, if one heated moment didn't arise then we weren't being real. That holiday was just what I needed. I had never had a holiday with friends before and it was one of the best holidays I have had. Thanks guys!

Having had time to think on holiday about what I was going to do, ramO and I sat on our trusted couch, the one that he had bought for £20 before I moved in with him in Banbury, and I rolled a spliff. It was time to create the future. I was going to go for it. I was going to offer multimedia marketing services. ramO had had enough of being ripped off by games companies and chose to offer business IT consultancy services for what would be our new company.

The next day, I set to work drawing up plans, developing ideas and then I opened up my email account, a Demon internet dial up account. Bear in mind folks, DVD at this time were still being developed and were only just being introduced to the larger companies and dial up internet was the norm in very few homes. I was just lucky I had married a techie geek… and what a lovely techie geek he is.

As I nipped downstairs to make a coffee little did I know that many of the customers I had left behind in my last job had contacted me annoyed that having finally been given a great, conscientious and efficient (their words not mine) account manager I had been taken away from them. They wanted me to do the work for them. As I continued to go through the emails, I came across emails from the suppliers from my previous employer saying pretty much the same thing. They wanted to either hire me or give me prices to rival those of my previous employer.

There was only one firm I called and I called them because I had become friends with Jules and I wanted to speak with her. Today we are still friends and she is living a life she loves in Greece.

I read these emails a few times over, drank more coffee and then sat on my bed. Then I lay down on my bed. My head was spinning. As I lay down on the bed I thanked God that the company I had worked for only had one email terminal for the whole company, Windows 3.1 (ramO and I were operating on Windows 95 at home) and no real artwork packages (again ramO and I had Corel Draw and an 'off site' copy of Photoshop). I had given all my clients my personal email address and mobile number just in case they needed to contact me about their orders out of hours; something colleagues had laughed at me about. They could email their artwork files to me; I would burn them to a CD and then take them into work ready for the next day. I had taught myself the artwork packages enabling me to spot mistakes and move their orders along swiftly. This way of thinking and doing business had paid off in dividends. It had cut out a lot of hard work building a client base, because I already had a large enough client base to keep me going, and to keep money coming in. I already had suppliers, knowledge of how to do the work and I already knew the mistakes made and holes in the services offered by competitors. My SWOT analysis was already completed.

I then decided to go and see the Princes Trust, the Chamber of Commerce and Business Link Thames Valley. None of them were prepared to help me. None of them gave me the advice they promised in the literature they had distributed across the city of Oxford so I had to do it by myself, with ramO. No worries. I went to a bookshop, looked in the business section and bought a few books on starting up in business, marketing a business and added them to my collection of sales and customer service books. One of the best books I have ever read on sales by the way is *The Great Sales Book* by Jack Collis – a fantastic book!

On my way back from Oxford City Centre I drove through Littlemore and through the Science Park looking for customers and as I was coming out I noticed a business centre – MWB Business Exchange. I went in, asked about rates and their services, asked for an information pack and went home.

The day had been productive so I rewarded myself with a spliff. I was sure ramO wouldn't mind if I had a cheeky one by myself. Taking the time to build the spliff, think about the day and what I had achieved I decided to make a really nice dinner for us both. If going to college and doing a course in Advanced Hospitality and Management had taught me one thing, it was how to cook a delicious meal. Training as a chef had been great fun, and had helped me understand my food issues a little more.

ramO came home and the house smelled wonderful. Not only was there a delicious meal ready and waiting for him, there was a spliff all for him. He laughed and told me he could get used to me working for myself if it meant he came home to a cooked meal like this every night and a wife buzzing her face off. I was not high from the spliff folks, that had brought me down from the clouds, I was high on pure adrenalin and motivation! Nothing was going to stop me now I had stepped off the treadmill of employment! I felt free, inspired, in control, excited. I felt as if I was going to explode with excitement. I was now working for myself and no one would ever be able to stop me. EVER! Dawnie was on a mission and all those goals I had written down in my journals would soon be ticked off. I gave myself a decade to tick off all of them. By the age of 30 I would have achieved all the goals I had set out for myself from the age of 16. Life was going to be great!

About a week after I had visited MWB Business Exchange, I was signing a contract on their smallest office. We couldn't really afford to have the office but the services and discounts we received by just being tenants there, we thought we would be able to pull it off.

Little did I know that I would meet two wonderful gentlemen by the names of James Arkle and Charles Lovibond[1], who would not only become mentors of mine but lifelong friends.

There are many people that will tell you not to take on the cost of an office at the beginning, and suggest staying at home in your spare room or kitchen table until you have out grown your home, but for me and my business mission, I had to be surrounded by people. I had to have that mental escape from the house. I needed to separate home and work, even though when I was at home, ramO and I would be discussing ideas, challenges and objectives.

I have my mother's workaholic trait. She works like a Trojan; she does everything from clean the toilet to manage her team. She is never prepared to ask someone else to do a job unless she does it herself, one of the many things I respect her for. My mother is my role model in work ethic, except I know now when to stop, something she has only just learnt to do now due to health reasons[2].

One thing my mother also taught me was to respect myself. This advice came in very handy when I received a phone call from a previous client, who I had asked my previous boss to either drop him as a client or give his account to someone else. My boss refused but now I was in the driving seat I could drop this guy and say what I had wanted to say to him for six whole months. This guy was a sleaze. He was married and had four children. He would request meetings on a Friday so we could have a meeting, have dinner and have 'a little bit of fun' together in the hotel that night. His account at the time was worth £250,000 per year and that day he promised to give me all of his other business, worth around £500,000, if I met him Friday and spent the night with him.

I felt violated. I was disgusted. Here was a married man older than my father offering me a £500,000 annual contract to sleep with him. I told him to stick his £500,000 up his backside, go home fix his marriage, find some self respect and learn to respect others. I told him he disgusted me and that I felt sorry for him. I also asked him how he dare disrespect my husband, me, his wife and his children in such an awful way. I also told him that if he was that desperate for sex, he should head down to Kings Cross and find a prostitute down there, who I am sure would only be too happy to sleep with him for £500 saving him £499,500. Seemed like a much better business deal to me. I also told him that if he ever called me again I would report him to the police and write to his local paper exposing him and his sleazy behaviour.

I put down the phone, walked out of my office and made a cup of tea; sat in the cafe area and thought about what I had just done. I felt proud of myself. I wanted to call my mum and tell her, but I knew she would be busy at work, so I didn't. I hoped she would be proud of me. I called ramO and told him. I just needed to talk to someone, but he was in a meeting. So I just kept it in and waited for ramO to call back; which he did some three hours later. He told me he was proud of me and then we both laughed. I had just said goodbye to a large amount of money and a contract that would have given us some nice profit margins, but I had kept my integrity and myself respect. I was not going to give up on those two things ever, because I firmly believe when you lose those, you sell out. You lose who you are.

Meeting James Arkle in the reception area of MWB later that same week was a blessing. He invited me to a 'networking' meeting. I remember telling him that my company didn't deal with computer networks, just software development and multimedia marketing[3]. He smiled at me and said, "Not that sort of network, this is a people's network." I was intrigued. My thinking was if this networking malarkey was as good as James said it was, and if it used the same principles that a computer network did of connecting people, sharing information fast and effectively and helping a business to run smoothly, then great. It would be just what I needed.

I went back to my office, called ramO and told him I was going to a networking meeting that night and I would be home about 9:30pm. Little did I know if the right people are in the meeting, the actual time the meeting ends would be much later! This wasn't due to mismanagement of time; it would simply be due to the chemistry in the room, the creation of ideas, business deals being done and discussed and too much fun being had to leave.

I arrived home about 11pm with my head spinning. I started telling ramO everything that had happened and who I had met and, and, and, and and... I was talking so quickly I nearly passed out! I had loved my first networking meeting and I had learnt so much.

So I joined this network called 'the missing Link' and looked forward to the meetings every week. They became part of my business diary and nine months later I decided to open up a missing Link network in Sheffield, the city ramO and I were moving to as it was 45 minutes away from three International airports and 20 minutes from the M1.

I was sad to leave Oxford but the idea of taking our business to the next level, an international level at that, was too exciting. Plus, it meant life would be much cheaper than living in Oxford. There were benefits all round to moving; just how many would not become clear for many years. With the opportunity of becoming a Director of a missing Link franchise, this would become our second business. ramO was hesitant at first but when I explained my thinking, he was fully on board. By paying for the franchise, not only would we have an income stream from membership, I would be able to use the meetings as an environment to learn from the other business owners at the meetings, and source deals for our main business. I would be able to penetrate the business community in Sheffield much quicker than if I simply joined other networks. Plus the format of the missing Link was new and refreshing. No one else networked like the missing Link networkers and soon we started to see chambers of commerce and other business networks copying the format. A compliment to say the least.

As my goal of owning a business was now in motion, I took the time to reflect on my other goals in life, mainly the one of becoming a better Muslim. I had started reading books about the life of the Prophet Mohammad and it was during this time that I found out his first wife Khadeeja was a businesswoman, his boss in fact. This was something that inspired me greatly and it gave me even more confidence. I was 21 years old, working in IT and Media and running my own business. There were many prejudices out there from the 'old boys' networks and a few times some of the so called big shot business men had requested I get them their coffee or tea, to which I simply told them I wasn't a waitress anymore and if they were getting themselves a hot drink I would have one too, a way of making up for the ignorant assumption they had just made about me. This won me a great deal of respect from many but annoyed those whose head was too far up their own backside. No loss, I only wanted to work with people I liked and who were open minded enough to see potential and opportunities in everyone. I knew I had a lot of potential and also a hell of a lot to learn. I was never too arrogant (I hope!) to deny that. If I made a mistake then I learnt quickly. I realised the more mistakes I made, the more I learnt. I guess it helped that I had the attitude that to admit you are wrong is to learn, whereas many people don't like to admit they are wrong.

So the move to Sheffield was nearly complete. Every time ramO and I had gone to Sheffield to visit his mum, we had taken a car load of boxes with us. It helped that at that time we had a VW Sharan and when the seats were taken out it made a great van, not to mention a great place to sleep after a night of raving! Yes we were still going out raving most weekends, but we had started to go to other clubs, such as The Fridge in Brixton, or Escape to Samara, and Passion in Coalville.

We still didn't miss a night at North at The Void and had now become part of the furniture, you could say. We had been raving with the North crew for nearly a decade and knew most of the DJs, MCs and club promoters. My favourite DJs at this point in time were three guys called Simon, Luke and Mark, and when two other guys called Jay or Sean MCed were with them it was wicked!

We visited Simon and Jay in Torquay, got to see Simon's studio – *how many buttons and sliding things? Ooo playtime!* Sadly for me Simon saw the glint in my eye and realised the sensible thing at this point was to distract me with a cuppa! I also got to ride pillion on Simon's brother's sexy motorbike along the sea front. I hadn't been on a motorbike since I had last been on my brother's motorbike. It felt great!

We chilled out with them a few times, but sadly not with Mark and his gorgeous missus Chrissi, who had become my crazy dancing friend; they were never in one place long enough for us to chill out together. We were always off to one end of the country whilst they were off to another.

Melly, Luke's partner, was always interesting to talk with. The thing I loved about Melly, and still do, is she is simply a really nice person, grounded, open minded and never seemed to bitch about anyone. With Melly, I always knew if she didn't speak, she either hadn't seen you, was wrapped up in her own thoughts or trying to help Luke, or one of the other guys sort themselves out behind the decks. I'm glad I got to meet her just as Melly and Dawn, not as ramO or Luke's Mrs. That always added another level to any conversation which I really didn't want to deal with. Melly had to deal with people only wanting to speak with her because of Luke's DJing, and I had to deal with being ramO's gold-digger girlfriend. Or I was too busy on the dance floor losing myself, and with my long wet hair pretty much covering my face most of the time, actually trying to see who was behind the decks was never really on my agenda.

I was there to dance. ramO and I had never really been impressed by the whole 'I'm not worthy' mindset so many have when it comes to DJs, MCs, promoters, or fellow business people. Everyone has a talent, the talent of these guys is simply to spin pieces of vinyl on turntables and create an amazing feeling in people that makes them want to dance. A great talent, but they work hard, extremely hard. They live and breathe their music. They all deserve the success they have had, but some of the other DJs got a little too big headed. Many of them (and their girlfriends/partners) played mind games and listened to other people's gossip too much.

Jay, our friend from the Diehard days was still banging out some good sets, but he was busy promoting his own events in Manchester. We would go along to those but as they were Saturday nights and we were normally in Wales by then getting our heads sorted for Monday morning, we didn't get to as many as we wanted to.

We had also lost a few friends by this point, things had happened or comments had been made that had shown either jealousy about ramO and I becoming business owners, or situations had not been fully understood and gossip had fuelled something out of control.

Around the time we moved to Sheffield, our friendship with Pete and Jill ended. This was heartbreaking. ramO had been friends with them for longer than he had known me, but unfortunately due to a situation with four other mutual friends at the time, they had not been privy to some vital information and got caught up in a catfight. Me being me decided to clear the air and explain how I felt, but due to my personal struggle with the issue that had caused the cat fight in the first place I couldn't, and wouldn't, disclose the issue. I simply felt that if they were good friends they would accept my decision and trust that when I was ready to share my struggle with the issue I would. This wasn't how it panned out though and the friendship ended. I was deeply hurt and so was ramO. He had just lost two of his friends because I wasn't ready to face a demon from my past and share it with anyone but him.

This break up in friendship led to others getting caught up in the gossip being fuelled by others and we saw a few of their friends fall by the wayside. ramO and I were just not prepared to discuss the issue with people uninvolved in the matter.

I don't like gossip and I don't like bitchiness. If I have something to say, I will say it to the person's face. If I discuss an issue, I discuss it as an issue and look at where I could have done things differently. I admit I didn't deal with the situation well, and ramO was upset with me about it, but with my head where it was, nothing but therapy many years later could solve it.

We were nine months in to our business, about to launch our second; we were moving home and times were stressful and we needed good friends around us, and would moreso in the coming months than we realised.

---

1. Though I would only get to meet Charles a year later after our move to Sheffield.
2. Because let's face it Mum, you are getting on a bit aren't you! xx
3. A rather a haphazard way of explaining my business at the time!

TEN

BABY'S BRAIN BLEEDS

I was woken up on Tuesday morning 8th May 2001 by ramO making loud disturbing noises. I thought he was dreaming to begin with so told him to be quiet. I noticed the time on the alarm clock and it said 6:03am. I was on holiday and not happy about being woken up so early. He carried on making the noises so I raised my voice and said, "Baby, it's 6:03, shut up! I want to sleep!" I rolled over to face him, and nothing could have prepared me for the sight I was about to witness for the next couple of hours…

We'd moved into our new home in Sheffield on April 27th. On Sunday 6th May ramO and I flew to Greece with Mum and Dad for a week's holiday. This was to be the first holiday I'd had with my parents since the age of 15. I was now 24. It was the first time I was going to spend more than a couple of days with them. I was nervous of how it was going to turn out, but I was looking forward to getting to know them on a different level. Spending time with them on neutral ground, away from the pressures of work, family gossip and reminders of the past would be good for us.

We arrived at our hotel late Sunday night, and on Monday morning we had breakfast together before exploring the local area. We had decided to spend some days together and others just as individual couples, meeting at the end of the day for dinner together. Whilst walking around the area, ramO and I came across a quad bike hire place and decided we would hire a couple of the bikes to go off around the Island on the Thursday. There were also a couple of Island tours we were considering, but would never get to go on, nor would we get to go on the quad bikes we were so excited about.

Now there was my Baby, my husband, my soul mate and partner in crime having a full on seizure[1]. To watch him even for those first initial seconds was frightening. I no longer wanted to sleep, I wanted to scream, but nothing came out at first. It felt as though someone had their hands around my throat. So many thoughts flashed through my mind, our future, our children that we were yet to have, his parents, my parents. So many emotions ran through my body; fear mainly but a deep sense of helplessness. None of the first aid training I had done in the past came to my mind other than don't try to restrain him. Not that I could have if I'd have tried. His body was convulsing in such a way it would have been impossible for me to even attempt it.

Finally, after what seemed like a lifetime, my parents came running in. I don't remember calling out to them, I don't remember screaming for them. I do remember crying and speaking to ramO letting him know that I was there. I remember seeing the door slightly open and seeing the trellis of beautiful red roses climbing up it, a thought of my nanny flashed into my head and a sense of being hugged came over me.

In this strange setting I felt safe; I knew things would be okay in the end. How long it would take to get there, I had no idea, but I just knew everything would work out okay. It had to. ramO and I had big plans for the future and we were determined to make them happen.

I remember looking over at the clock and it was now 6:24am… surely the clock was wrong? ramO was now coming out of the convulsions and was starting to lie calmly on the bed.

I was about to go over to him to stroke his head when he suddenly sprang onto all fours and looked at me as if he didn't know who I was. He looked really confused. He didn't know what was going on, something I expected, but seeing him with no recollection of who I was, made my whole body go weak. I wanted to fall to the floor in a heap; I didn't know how much longer I could stand for. He looked scared and lost; and he had a really intense look on his face.

As I stepped forward slowly to put my hand on his shoulder, he leapt on all fours to the opposite diagonal corner of the twin beds we had pushed together. In that instant, he reminded me of the cavemen you see in science programmes and movies that show you how early man moved about on all fours. I heard a gasp from those in the room and I felt my throat get tighter and tighter. I felt as though someone was strangling me. My eyes were burning with tears that I would not let fall. I had to be strong; he could not see me fall apart. My husband needed me more now than ever, even though he didn't know who I was.

The next few hours passed in a big blur. After ramO had calmed down, I remember a couple of men come in and place him on a stretcher and load him into the back of a white transit van, the local ambulance. I remember my Mum and Dad talking to the hotel owners. I remember being offered a cup of tea. I remember the very bumpy road to the hospital and the hospital room being a terracotta type orange colour. There were several doctors around him at the end of the room of four beds. There was a toilet at the beginning of the room. There was one small window which didn't offer anything other than a view of another wall. The heart monitor and brain monitor that ramO was hooked up to reminded me of a really old dot matrix printer that had two bare metal wires twisted around a little knob which was then connected to something resembling an ear drops pipette sucker which managed to attach itself to his chest, and to the top and sides of his head. I remember being in what appeared to be a corridor next to a surgical theatre-come-examination room. There was a strong smell of bleach and disinfectant, no bacteria was ever going to survive the smell let alone the actual liquids that was for sure.

The next thing I remember is being back in the hotel sitting on the bed next to ramO. He was lying in my Mum and Dad's bed in their room. He looked so tired and when he woke up it took him a while to realise who I was, for a split second I wondered if he would ever know who I was again. Then I saw his eyes warm to me and his recognition came back. The first words he said were the most magical words he has ever uttered to me, "Baby. Hmmm. Look at you." He didn't know where he was and he had no idea what had happened, I couldn't bring myself to tell him, I just told him he was asleep in Mum and Dad's bed, which he accepted.

He then asked for some food and a drink so we went to the cafe/bar beside the pool where Mum and Dad were sitting watching the football. Liverpool FC were playing so ramO made himself comfortable with a smile on his face[2]. He was still really tired and not entirely sure of what had happened. The hospital had pumped him full of anticonvulsant drugs, so his mind was numb... a very different kind of reaction than to the drugs we were both used to. The main thing was he was up and about and wanting to eat. Mum, Dad, ramO, and I were all sat eating when, all of a sudden, my Mum got up and left the table in tears. Dad and I looked at each other and wondered what had upset Mum, ramO told me to go after her to make sure she was okay and so I did. I didn't really want to leave him but he seemed to be okay.

I went after my Mum. I found her on her bed sobbing her eyes out. I sat down beside her and put my arm around her and asked what the matter was. I was not ready for what came next. My Mum just looked at me and said, "You just can't help yourself can you. You are always trying to come between me and your Dad!"

Stunned and hurt by what my mum had just said, these words come out, "What? What are you saying? Why do you keep saying this? We were all just sat eating nicely together and, after everything that has just happened, you come out with this? What is wrong with you?" Looking back now, I still don't understand why my Mum said this, but we didn't have time to finish the conversation.

My Dad came running in and said, "ramO's off again."

I bolted out of the door and saw my Baby having a stronger convulsion that the one he had had that very same morning. I moved the chairs and tables out of the way and the people in the bar were just stood there, we all were, waiting for the seizure to stop. I remember looking at the TV screen and saw that Liverpool had lost, a little chuckle escaped in my mind due to my sense of humour thinking a seizure was a little over the top just because Liverpool had lost. A joke I would later share with my Baby when he came around again. He would appreciate the joke.

The time on the TV screen said 9:30pm, hadn't it only just been 8:20pm?

A couple in their 50s walked past the cafe/bar and I heard them say, "Young ones today, taking all these drugs and over drinking, look at the mess they get themselves into!"

I flew into a rage. I screamed, "How the fuck do you know what is going on here? He is ill; this has nothing to do with drink or drugs! How dare you and your small minds comment on something you know nothing about!"

I then heard my mum saying, "Dawn Louise! Calm down, don't speak to those people like that!"

"Calm down! You want me to calm down? How can you expect me to calm down? And why are you asking me not to speak like this when it is them with their ignorant comments who should be told not to speak in that way? You always defend others; it would be nice if you'd defend me for once!"

ramO was still going for it on the floor, the ambulance was still not there, and the atmosphere in the air was very heavy. We stood at the entrance to the hotel grounds looking up into the hills for the ambulance.

The time was 10:41pm when the ambulance finally arrived. It arrived with no head lights and this time it was more of a pickup truck with the detachable hood attached to it. Inside were the wooden benches I used to balance across in gymnastics at school with a metal pole to hold onto behind me. The bed ramO was lying on was clipped into place to make sure it didn't roll out of the truck. I promised never to moan about the NHS again. Us Brits don't know how lucky we have it, we really don't.

I don't remember arriving at the hospital, I don't remember being set up in the room we had seen only that morning. Doctors kept talking to me, but in Greek. I had no idea what they were saying to me or what was happening. All I know is they had given ramO loads of medication and before me lay my Baby sleeping peacefully. It was then I looked around the room, the room we were going to be staying in until we were flown back to the UK.

Good old Thomas Cook travel insurance. ramO had said it was a waste of time taking it out, but for £25 I was not going to risk it. Thank God I had taken it out, and that ramO valued my opinion, not to mention couldn't give me one objection I couldn't overcome! Thank Goodness for all the sales training I had had years before!

I must have fallen asleep, because I remember waking up due to a pain in my left cheek. I had fallen asleep on the metal bar along the side of the bed, the one that my Baby was strapped to just in case he had another seizure. I looked around the room. There were three other men in the room, one looked so weak and ill I didn't know if he would make it through the night, the other two look very malnourished but had a twinkle in their eyes none the less. They were not really with it and I just assumed they were under the influence of medicinal drugs.

A little while later I was proven right. The nurses came in with morphine. These were the biggest nurses I had ever seen. They could bed bath these men in no time at all, something I would see a lot more of over the next week as they had trouble controlling their toilet movements. Not pleasant for me or for them.

I must have fallen asleep again because I was woken up by a nurse bringing breakfast to everyone, except me. Having looked at it, I was glad they hadn't brought me anything. It looked like cloudy frogspawn, but it had a sweet taste to it and an oaty smell so when ramO woke up and said he was hungry, I fed him his frogspawn. He had trouble eating because he had bitten his tongue and lips quite badly. It was like feeding a baby. The frogspawn went everywhere, but I managed to get half of it down him. He didn't like the orange juice because it stung his mouth so I offered to go and get him some water.

As I left the room, I don't know where I thought I was going, or where I thought I could get water from. There were posters on the wall with pictures of toilets asking guests and patients not to flush toilet roll down the toilet. There were people smoking in the hospital, including the doctors. Mobile phones were being used by everyone I could see.

The walls started spinning around me and the next thing I know I am outside in a courtyard overlooking the town of Zanti. It was such a sunny day. The sun felt warm on my face and then I just remember crying. Then laughing. Then crying. I had no idea what was going on but I just kept thinking of how lucky we were to be together and to have God. I said a prayer overlooking Zanti for ramO, the men in the room and for all those suffering from illness and loneliness. I took a deep breath and went to find the entrance back into the hospital.

The next thing I remember is sitting in an armchair at the end of my Baby's bed, which I am sure was not there before, watching him sleep.

Then I was sat beside his bed in the most uncomfortable chair probably known to man, holding his hand, whilst texting like a mad woman to our friend Rich in the UK. He had been the only one to reply to the text message I had obviously sent out, something I don't remember doing. Without his support and words of encouragement I would have found that time in my life really hard.

I saw my parents maybe twice more for about an hour each time over the next week. Their thinking was, why should they let this ruin their holiday, and they were right. Why should they? There was not enough room for them in the hospital anyway, and it would have been a waste of money if they had not explored and had fun. None of us knew what was going to happen, or when ramO and I were being flown back to the UK, so them being within easy reach of the hotel where a Thomas Cook holiday representative could speak to them was a good thing.

I really needed them by my side, I wanted them to be by my side, but I had got used to being by myself so, I just accepted they were on holiday to enjoy themselves.

The next few days ramO lay in bed like a zombie, the wrist straps had been removed once they had got the drug dose right and were sure he wouldn't have another seizure. I remember more frogspawn arriving, more bed baths for the men in the room and more doctors and nurses trying to talk to me to explain what was happening but not having a clue.

Then after a few days a holiday representative from Thomas Cook arrived and said the doctors had arranged with them to fly us home that day. She told me we had been in the hospital for six days and they were sorry we had had to stay there that long, but the doctors wanted to make sure it was safe to fly.

We were flying home the same day we were meant to fly home on, but we flew first class with a doctor. It wasn't a very large plane, nor was it really first class, but we were flying home: me and my sexy zombie. We flew over Athens. It looked beautiful and I promised one day to return.

We arrived at Manchester airport and were greeted by a paramedic in green overalls and a radio, a far cry from the greasy mechanic looking chap that had driven the pickup truck in Zanti.

ramO was put into a wheelchair, and then placed onto a hospital bed inside the ambulance. His heart was being monitored, as was his brain activity. He had an oxygen mask over his face and I held his hand.

I was glad to be heading back to Sheffield, especially as we were driving via the Snake Pass with its beautiful mountain views, streams and waterfalls.

The paramedic was radioing the Royal Hallamshire Hospital in Sheffield, informing them of the heart and brain readings, the medication we had brought with us, and it was all blurring into each other.

What is normally an hour's journey felt like five minutes and as soon as we arrived at the Royal Hallamshire, ramO was taken off into an examination room, and I was told to sit down, have a cup of tea and something to eat.

That cup of tea was wonderful and I did not realise it at the time but I had not eaten anything for about two days, and even then all I had eaten was a sandwich from the hospital. The team at the Hallamshire also gave me some 'scrubs' to change into after a shower. I had not showered in a few days and I needed to shower and change.

I stayed at the hospital until ramO was moved up to the M ward and then the hospital staff sent me home to get some sleep. I arrived home, walked upstairs to bed and fell asleep until the next morning.

Somewhere in amongst all of the above, I had called my father-in-law as well as Janny and Alexs. I thought it would be best if my father-in-law called and spoke to my mother-in-law to explain what had happened. He was a doctor, his English was better so he'd understand better from me and be able to explain in Arabic for my mother-in-law to understand fully what was going on. I also knew he would call the Hallamshire hospital and speak with some of his friends and colleagues who'd worked with him there to find out the true situation, doctor to doctor.

I was right. He did call them and he arrived in the UK a couple of weeks later to be with me and ramO. Janny and Alexs arrived from Wales a couple of days after I arrived home in Sheffield to be with me. I will never forget them being there for me. Without them there I would have gone to pieces. They kept me strong. They showed me true friendship by taking time off work to be with me. Something I wished I would have been able to do for them, but I never got the chance.

It was a crazy time. ramO was in hospital, I was already operating our existing business in Sheffield, renovating the house, and developing the missing Link, ready to be launched in September. I had orders to fulfil and so my days were extremely busy.

I would wake up in the morning, either go to the gym or straight to the office.

At lunchtime I would then go and visit ramO in hospital, he wasn't really with it but I told him about the new orders, the completed orders, how the launch was going, what was happening with the builders and how the new bathroom suite had arrived, and how even though the bath was in the lounge, I hoped to be having a relaxing bath by the weekend.

The hour-long visit would fly by, and then it would be back to the office for a couple of hours before heading off to the gym for either a swim or a spinning session.

I remember being in one of Elise's (Elise Marie Lindsay) spinning classes. I could hear her voice, I could hear her ramping us up for a climb, but then I remember her voice zoning out. I felt tears falling down my face, my legs slowing down and my gaze just going off into the distance. I don't know whether I stopped pedalling but I had just spun out big time. Disorientation filled my entire mind, with so many thoughts crashing into my head; I had brought a whole new version of spinning to Greens Gym! No one mentioned anything to me after the class but I do know that something must have happened because one of the other spinning teachers Ian Cooper decided to make fun of me the next spinning class I went to. I laughed it off, I knew he didn't mean any harm, and I know that had he known what was happening in my life at that moment, he wouldn't have said anything. Something which was proven months later whilst Ian, the twins and I were in our Friday morning rowing class. One of the twins asked me if I was the one whose husband had been ill in hospital, when I said yes, Ian looked shocked and embarrassed. He, nor I, ever said anything, but his little wink every time he saw me after that spoke volumes.

He came across as a tough guy, but he was a good guy deep down.

I know that during this time so much was happening but I just had to keep focused. When I arrived back at the hospital the next day, I was told by Mr Battersby, the lead consultant, that ramO had what they called an Arterio-Venuous Malformation (AVM) in his brain. It was a type of tumour that affected the veins or arteries, it was congenital, and one in 200 people have them; most go undetected. The AVM haemorrhaged and bled into his brain and that had resulted in his seizures. It was a large AVM and would need removing. Plans were going to be made to remove it, but they wanted to make sure he was strong enough to cope with the surgery. They needed to operate.

Mr Battersby then left the room and one of the other doctors told me to prepare myself, ramO might not make it. I had better speak with the solicitors and make arrangements. I told him everything was going to be fine, he didn't know my husband like I knew him and if anyone was going to survive this then he was.

I got in the car to drive home, and as I was driving along Brocco Bank towards Hunters Bar roundabout, my mobile rang. I answered it thinking it was the hospital but it turned out to be Pete, one of the friends we had fallen out with a month or so before. I told him I couldn't talk at that moment and asked if he could call me back, but instead of listening to me, he just went off his head at me. He started shouting down the phone about how he was calling about his friend, and who the fuck did I think I was? He wanted to come and visit and, as always, I was being childish and turning all ramO's friends against him.

Tears came rolling down my face again. I had just left the hospital after having a really difficult conversation about my husband possibly not making it. I was five minutes from home, all Pete had to do was wait 10 minutes before calling back, and we could have made the arrangements for him to come and visit ramO. But no, he flew off the handle like he had done before, without all the facts, and being so insensitive and nasty. He didn't realise it was this kind of behaviour that had started to make ramO second guess their friendship.

I wasn't going to tell ramO what had just happened, he didn't need to know. I got home, washed my face, made myself a coffee and called Pete back. He rejected the call about three times.

I knew then the friendship was over for good. I couldn't allow myself to be friends with someone who was that insensitive.

I had other things to focus on as well. I was operating the business, the house was nearly finished. The new windows were in, the new kitchen and floors were in and the decorators had finished their work too. All that was needed was the bath and shower to be fitted. The mosaic tiling was taking the time but I knew it would look good when it was finished. It would be worth it, and oh how I longed for a long hot soak in the bath. All the furniture was in the right rooms, some pieces just needed switching round and the curtains were up too. Now it was time to unpack all the boxes properly.

Over the next week ramO improved so much. The doctors had got the medication dose sorted out and he was showing signs of improvement, like I knew he would.

ramO came home from hospital 12 days after we landed in the UK, a few days after Janny and Alexs left to go back to Wales. Their help had been amazing.

I remember once ramO was home, he sat in the arm chair in the lounge, with the bath beside him, and he was just like a zombie, but he was my zombie and he was home. That is all that mattered. He then said something and I cannot for the life of me think what it was, but I knew what he said hurt me deeply. I threw a tantrum a three-year-old would have been proud of, and I fell to the floor sobbing. I was exhausted. I was mentally, emotionally and physically drained. He picked me up off the floor, sat me on his knee and we hugged each other so tightly. I needed that hug *so* much. I needed to feel his strong arms around me. We sat there like that for ages, and then we went upstairs to bed and fell asleep in each other's arms until the morning.

---

1. I found out later the medical term is a "grand mal seizure".
2. He'd always supported Liverpool, and still does, even though they're nearly as bad as Middlesbrough nowadays … sorry baby, couldn't resist :)

ELEVEN
11TH SEPTEMBER

It was now some months since ramO had come home from hospital. He had been taken off one of the drugs he was given: Tegretol. He was so angry and aggressive whilst he was on this drug. He switched to Phenytoin and was to remain on it for the rest of his life.

He had felt useless at home, so he had started coming into the office with me to make himself useful. It was great having him there, other than the fact that I could no longer play my music because he couldn't concentrate on the tasks he was working on.

The seizures had caused a little bit of brain damage to a part of his brain that enabled him to focus. He would probably find it difficult to focus on more than one task at a time. I joked that he was a man, what would be the difference. The doctors hadn't appreciated this humour unfortunately. But it was humour that had got us through most of the hard times over the last few months. I told ramO about how he had the second seizure whilst Liverpool were losing, and how I had fed him frogspawn.

The best bit of humour came from our friend Rob Gob. He had come to visit from Manchester and whilst we were all joking around, he said, "I bet if we'd put some Loftgroover on, you'd have been banging in time with the music! Hahaha! Nice one!" When he first said it, I was a bit shocked but then I saw the funny side and whenever I felt down after that, I would always remember what Rob said. It would always bring a smile to my face. My mother-in-law had also arrived from Egypt with my brother-in-law 3Emad. This was to be challenging, not just because of our difficult relationship (I wasn't an Egyptian woman for a start!), but also because she had not seen the changes we had made to the house in Sheffield.

ramO had been asked to do some work for a very large client up in Glasgow. It was a hard decision to make but he felt he was up for it, and he needed to prove to himself he could continue with his software analysis and development.

I was a bit of a wreck the whole time he was away. When he didn't call the moment he said he would, I would be pacing up and down wondering if he had had another seizure, if he was lying face down in the gutter or had been taken to hospital. He didn't like me worrying but we both knew I would do, and we both knew that sometimes it just isn't possible to call when you say you will. It didn't make it any easier though.

His mother was angry because she had come to take care of him and he had gone to Glasgow, and it was my fault (obviously!) and she found so many faults with the new design of the house, all of which were just picky things. Even though I understood her being possessive over the house, she had told us to make it our home.

I was still under immense pressure getting ready for the launch of the missing Link at the beginning of September, that when she and 3Emad left, I was relieved. I could just get on and do what was needed to be done without worrying about having to rush home to be the dutiful daughter-in- law.

I had attended pretty much every networking event in Sheffield and promoted the launch through all the media avenues I had come to know. Every business in every business centre had been given an invite and it was now the day of the launch of the Missing Link South Yorkshire, it was 11th September 2001.

Before I had time to call everyone to confirm their attendance that night, people were calling me to find out if the event was still on. I was impressed that they were keen to call me. Normally the organiser has to call all the guests to make sure they were still attending. I thought to myself, *Wow, I like this attitude to events, maybe this is going to be easier than I thought it would be.* How very little I knew. I had been so busy planning the catering, organising the printed materials, organising the meeting agendas, feedback forms, referral forms and the membership application forms for the event, that I had no idea what was going on in the big wide world that day!

At 6pm, James, Charles, and Matt arrived from Oxford; it was a huge relief to see them. I had heard so much about Charles and I was excited to meet him. His reputation definitely preceded him and it was an impressive reputation to have, so much so, I was a little intimidated!

They went up to the room, settled themselves and I made sure the teas and coffees were being put on by Claire the receptionist of the Sheffield Science Park[1].

The catering arrived just after 6pm, and everyone else started to arrive from 6:45pm. I was at the front door to greet everyone and direct them to the meeting room.

Once the last guest was ticked off my list and I locked the doors, I went up to the bathroom, washed my face, touched up my makeup and went into the meeting room.

What greeted me, surprised me. Everyone was completing a minute's silence. Who had died? I was not to find out until after the meeting!

The meeting went well, everyone enjoyed themselves, contacts were made and I felt it had been a success; more importantly so did James. He was proud of me for everything I had achieved. Charles gave me a huge hug and told me, "Well done you, you should be very proud of yourself." I was.

I had pulled off a successful launch, established our company ABL on the Sheffield Business scene, renovated a three-bedroom house and dealt with my husband's health issue all in the space of six months. I was shattered.

Once the congratulations were over and done with, I asked them why they had been doing a minute's silence at the beginning of the meeting. James couldn't help but chuckle to himself and mention the 'Dawnie Bubble'.

Whilst I had been running around making sure everything for the meeting had gone well, 'some terrorists' had flown an aeroplane into each of the twin towers in New York.

So I cleared the boardroom with the help of the Oxford boys, said good night and went home.

I switched on the TV and poured myself a glass of non-alcoholic wine. The world was about to get a whole lot crazier for the foreseeable future. Little did we know just how crazy.

The next few months were very tense. I was married to an Arab, we were both Muslims. I was not wearing a headscarf at this point so I got to hear the true views people held about Muslims, Pakistanis and Arabs. Even though no proof had come to light just who had done it there were many accusations. A lot of anti Arab feeling had died down, but the anti-Muslim feeling was intensifying. It was very interested to hear the many different viewpoints of the people within the Sheffield business community, as well as the community at large.

Sometimes there would be some of the most aggressive things I have ever heard in my life coming out of people's mouths. Sometimes, I would walk into a room and the room would go quiet, normally because there was one or two in the room that knew I was a Muslim. There were very few who were the voices of reason and even fewer who said, "If America wasn't such a global bully, this would not have happened."

I kept my views, for once, to myself. It was safer for me to do so, and as I didn't really know anything about this Al Qaeda group, or the Pakistanis in Sheffield, I wasn't prepared to comment. How could I? If I had my comments would have been ignorant ones. The views I did have, and did share, were simple ones, "You cannot hold all Muslims and Pakistanis accountable for the actions of a few, just as you cannot blame all Catholics for the paedophilia that many of the priests in the Catholic churches were starting to be accused of. There are 'nut-jobs' and twisted people in every faith, non faith and walk of life. To accuse everyone that belongs to a certain faith is stupidity." Many agreed, many just refused point blank to accept simple logic, even when given other analogies. Their racism, prejudices and anger were set far too deep for anything to change their minds.

Following the events of September 11th, the missing Link started to grow in membership, ABL started to win new clients from the surrounding area, across the UK and across Europe. We were doing okay.

We took on a member of staff called Leiza and she was a great addition to the team. She had to deal with a lot though. Not only were ramO and I growing the business, we had his impending surgery coming up. We had been given the choice between open brain surgery, where the risks of opening up his skull and brain to remove the tumour posed huge risks, and would create greater brain damage, but would remove the tumour 100% for sure; or we could try Stereotactic radio-surgery, AKA the Gamma Knife. It would mean a gamma laser would be used to 'remove' the tumour by blasting it with gamma radiation, and then we would have to wait for two more years to see if the surgery had worked and the tumour had gone[2].

We opted for The Gamma Knife surgery. A date was set for the surgery after which we'd take a holiday to Melbourne, Australia to see Ferdi. We would also be going to Sydney for my birthday in the December.

The build up to the operation was intense. Would ramO make it through the surgery, would he not? If he didn't, what was I going to do? I couldn't imagine my life without him. What about my baby ramO? Would I ever be able to have his children? The next time we went to the hospital for his blood tests, I asked about methods to ensure I was able to have his children. We would be able to freeze his sperm and then when I was ready to have a child, all I would have to do, is let them know and then the procedure would begin. My dream of having his baby would be able to come true.

The public opinion of Muslims was becoming worse and worse. I found myself defending a group of people I didn't know anything about. The only Muslims I knew were ramO, ramO's family, and a couple of friends. They were all very kind people. I knew enough about Islaam to know that it did not promote the negative rumours being spread amongst the red top tabloid press readers and the Daily Mail/Express readers.

The local press seemed to only run stories about Muslim gang fights in certain parts of the city and one local journalist even went as far as wearing a black gown, headscarf and face veil 'to see what it was like'. A pretty stupid stunt if you asked me because she would never know what it is like because she hadn't chosen to wear it for the right reasons. Any interactions or events that would happen during this stunt would be tainted with her own ideas and feelings, not those of a Muslim woman who had chosen to wear it as a symbol of her faith (or culture).

I had no connection to the Muslim community at all, and if the events in America on September the 11th did anything, it drove me and many more people, both Muslim and non Muslim, onto a quest to find out more about these 'scary terrorists' that plagued the world and, not to mention, stole all the jobs AND the benefits in the UK.

---

ramO was taken to hospital in the November for his surgery, with me and his dad in tow. We were first led into a room where everything that was about to happen was explained to us.

First he would have this metal helmet type thing that looked like a salad colander screwed into his skull, after which he would be wheeled into the Gamma Knife room for surgery.

Once inside the room, he would then be asked to lie down on the bed where the colander would be screwed into the frame which would keep his head in place. He had been asked prior to the day if there was any music he wanted to listen to whilst he was in the Gamma machine. He had chosen to listen to our friend Alex 'Bluey'. The CD would be played whilst he was inside the machine and the Gamma Knife Laser penetrated his brain where the tumour was. This whole procedure would take a few hours. I could wait inside the surgery or I could go and wait in a waiting room.

The first part of the procedure was the screwing in of the colander into his skull. The noise of the metal screwdriver against the bone of his skull was awful and I can still hear it today when I think about it. ramO being ramO decided this was a great photo opportunity and pulled out his trusty camera and handed it to me. I was feeling rather faint but didn't let on whilst I took the photos from the side and from the back. As soon as I stood in front of him to take a picture, I was rumbled.

"Ah Baby, bless you! Hahaha! Look how pale you are! Hmm you're so funny!"

The medical assistant had to take over because at the moment I saw the screwdriver go into his skull and the first bolt going in, I am not sure if I passed out or not, but I don't remember the rest of them going in, that's for sure! I do remember the walk to the gamma theatre and seeing the big machine. I didn't watch them screw his head to the bed, I was sat with the surgeons who were about to operate the joystick.

I was really nervous. How could they remove this tumour with what looked like an Atari VCS joystick[3]? I was then asked to leave so the surgery could start; I was really pleased about this. I had some work to do at the office and so I left the hospital and busied myself; which proved pointless because I never got anything done at all. I just wandered around in a daze. I collected ramO's dad and we went to the hospital ready for ramO to come out of surgery.

As soon as I saw him in his bed on the ward, I knew he had had another grand mal seizure[4]. His dad and I looked at each other and I saw the depth of his father's strength. He transformed from a worried father to a concerned doctor within seconds. How he pushed the doctor in front of his role of a father I will never know. My respect for him in that moment grew in abundance. I always knew he was strong, but to see him in those moments transformed my view of him and created a bond between us that can only be created in moments like that. Moments later ramO had another seizure and we were both ushered out of the room for the doctors to deal with it.

When we finally arrived home that night, I lay in bed thinking about everything that had happened to me since I had met ramO. I thought about my life before him. The dreams I had created; the goals I had set myself and the amount of opportunities that had come my way.

It was strange to look at my life and reflect in this calm way when my husband lay in bed in hospital 10 minutes away recovering from brain surgery and yet another seizure. Everything I had planned to happen had happened. Everything I had wanted to achieve had been achieved. Yes things had been difficult, and yes things were scary right now, but I felt this resolve come over me that no matter what happened in the next 48 hours, I would honour every promise I had ever made to ramO. I would go on to fulfil all the goals we had set for ourselves and our future children. I would have my baby ramO; I would make sure our business was a success. I would move to Egypt to teach the children about the Arab culture and we'd all learn the language. I would honour him always, as I had promised to do; and I would honour myself by being the woman that he knew I could become... even if I had no idea how to do it, all our goals and dreams would come true. I was now on the craziest mission of my life and no matter what happened it would be a successful mission. Houston, we have lift-off!

---

1. God only knows what I would have done without Claire over those past six months!
2. The consultants explained that no one really knew how the gamma radiation got rid of the tumour's cells, but when it worked the tumour would literally vanish!
3. The original games console.
4. Grand mal seizures are the worst type of seizure, and ramO only seemed to have them, but then again, he did always like top of the range!

TWELVE

BECOMING A MOTHER

ramO came out of this third seizure okay. It was only a short, five minute, seizure compared to the 30-plus minute ones he had had in Greece, and according to the doctors and consultants, it was to be expected after major brain surgery.

He had another seizure whilst we were at the hospital the next day and I was beginning to think the trip to Australia we had chosen to go on to see Ferdi and get some much needed rest would never happen. But after several days, the doctors released ramO from hospital and gave him the all clear to fly. Not only was I relieved to hear that he was okay, I was also relieved to know that the 22-hour flight ahead of us was not going to be a problem. We needed to get away. We needed to get away from the house, the business, the hospital and the reminders of the last eight months. Australia was about as far away as we could go, so we set off.

Arriving in Australia and seeing Ferdi was a mixture of relief and joy. I was glad that there had been no complications on the flight due to the surgery, and just pleased to have arrived in Australia to see Ferdi, and see the country. Not that we would get to see much of this huge country as we were only there for a couple of weeks. We were going to be based in Melbourne, with a few days in Sydney for my birthday, but we could make a start.

I had always wanted to go to Donovans restaurant in Melbourne ever since I had heard about it many years before, so going there was a must, and it didn't disappoint. Everything I wanted it to be and more; beautiful food, great service and a homely, yet elegant all at the same time.

Whilst in Sydney ramO and I climbed the Sydney Harbour Bridge, although it wasn't proper climbing in the way I had imagined, but it was still good to do it.

We visited the Melbourne Museum and I filled in the gaps of my knowledge regarding 'all those criminals' the British Government had sent to Australia generations before.

It was sad to see so little history of the Aborigines, but after the full two weeks of being in Melbourne, seeing the way in which people behaved towards the Aborigines, I started to understand why there was none of their history in the museum, and the depths of racism in this part of the world. There was so much of it I felt dirty just being there. How can people be so nasty and ignorant?

ramO and I spent most of the time at night smoking joints, which helped to stop the white noise he was experiencing in his head[1], and the constant chatter in mine, and we just chilled.

Things were not the same with Ferdi as they had been in the UK. We had been through a lot and as a result had changed so much, appreciating things in a way that only an experience such as ours could teach someone. Ferdi had been told the gossip about what had supposedly happened between Pete, Jill, ramO and I. Ferdi asked why it had happened and it was obvious she had been told things of little substance or actual fact, but just half truths based on a total lack of information and understanding. The disappointing thing was, she had made up her mind about our friendship before we had even arrived in Australia. It was over before we had even arrived. This was further confirmed on one of our last mornings in the country whilst ramO was sleeping and I was cleaning my teeth. I overheard a conversation whilst everyone thought ramO and I were asleep, about how mixed race couples are disgusting and shouldn't be allowed. The conversation between Ferdi and her friends hurt me deeply. How could she, after all the kindness we had shown her whilst she was in the UK, think like this and then allow these kinds of ignorant, racist comments be made about ramO and I, and our future 'abnormal, disadvantaged' children.

I remember standing in the bathroom, tears falling down my face. She had been like my younger sister. She had lived with us for eight months, gone everywhere with us, we'd helped her find a job and introduced her to the many friends she still has to this day in the UK. The betrayal was awful. The irony was one of her friends had aboriginal heritage so not only had she betrayed me and her friend, but her friend had also betrayed her own family!

I put my toothbrush down, washed my face and then calmly walked into the front lounge and told them all what I thought of their ignorant, racist views, and how I was glad to be leaving in a few days. The thought of spending more time in their company disgusted me. I couldn't say anything to Ferdi; I was hurting so much I just stared at her. I didn't even want to be near her.

Nothing else was said and I went back into the bedroom to be with the only person I felt safe with, ramO. How could things have turned out like this? Why did people think this way? Why do people listen to gossip and allow it to damage friendships and other people's lives? I lay there next to ramO thinking about all the challenges I had had in my life. All the ignorance in the world, all the hatred and I just wanted to make it all go away. As I lay there next to my wonderful, amazing husband just staring at him, I realised I was crying. I didn't want to wake him so I made sure I swallowed my tears. My conversations with God for the next hour were ones of, "What lessons are there in this for me? What are you trying to show me? How am I going to get through all this?"

Then a thought came to me, ever since the first two weeks of knowing ramO, all I had wanted were his babies. I made a decision, whilst lying on the bed next to him, that I was going to come off the pill. I wanted ramO's babies and nothing was going to stop me. I couldn't risk losing him forever, so having his babies was, in my mind, the only way he would live on if he did die on me.

I also made the choice that my children were never going to be raised in ignorance. They were going to travel the world and meet people from every walk of life and ethnicity. If I was going to be part of a solution, then I had to raise my children to think differently to the nasty ignorant people that Ferdi surrounded herself with. They had to realise that people are the same; their bodies have just evolved to cope with different weather and physical differences around the globe. It doesn't make them something to be feared, or ridiculed. God made us all the same, equal.

Later that day, after all Ferdi's friends had left, the tension was still high between us. I wanted to get out of the beach house, so we went for a walk along the beach. Whilst walking on the beach, I pulled out my pill packet[2] and got down on my hands and knees. I asked God to forgive me for littering and then buried the packet deep in the sand. I prayed we would be blessed with a mini ramO soon, and that I would become a great mummy. I wanted to bury the pain, hand it all over to God and leave it all behind in Australia[3].

My friendship with Ferdi was hanging by a thread, but I still loved her. I knew deep down the Ferdi I knew in the UK was still in there, and prayed that one day she would surface again. Boarding the plane, I said goodbye not just to Ferdi, but to the holiday we had in Greece and the months that had followed. I said goodbye to the many problems I had with my family. I said goodbye to what had gone before and fell asleep thinking of the life that now laid ahead, the life of embracing motherhood.

Four months later, ramO and I sat waiting for the blue line. Were we pregnant with our first child? We were so excited. Deep down I knew I was, but the fear of being wrong was too much. That minute was the longest minute I can remember. We sat together holding hands and each of us held one end of the pregnancy test. We kept looking each other, kissing each other and then when that little blue line appeared, we just giggled together and kissed. It was magical. I thanked God so much and made a promise to Him, to our unborn child and to ramO, to be the best mummy I could be. To learn about parenting the same way I would learn about any new skill or task I undertook. Listen to my gut instinct, but read as many theories as I could, without losing the practicalities of the task. I didn't want to mess up my children's heads or hearts, because the damage could last a life time, and let's face it, there are too many messed up people in this world.

Throughout the pregnancy I kept a diary of my thoughts, feelings and basically had conversations with our unborn child. Neither ramO nor I wanted to know the sex of the baby, and we had already chosen two boys' names and two girls' names years before, but I knew the baby would be Khaalid and I couldn't wait to meet him. I knew that he would be a lover of music by the way he started moving when I put music on. He especially enjoyed Mark EG and Metallica, great taste already. I kept working on the business every day and it was nice to have many of our colleagues as excited as we were, especially Steven and Sandra.

Over that year, the four of us had become good friends. We all had a daft sense of humour, hints of sarcasm and we all loved improving ourselves and our communities. Business was good and through our work, we all got to spend a lot of time together. One of the things I loved about the friendship we had with Steven and Sandra is the fact that we could just 'be' with each other, we didn't have to say anything to fill the time, had a rant if we wanted to (and that was mainly just me!) and we all had different views on many things. I loved the fact that just between the four of us there were five languages spoken – my contribution was sadly lacking as I only spoke English[4] – and four cultures shared, Steven being Flemish and Sandra being German, not including the subcultures of the respective countries we had lived in.

One of the things that really helped me during the pregnancy was the emotional support from both of them. Still not being close to my mum, and not having her with me through the pregnancy, I felt very down, but Sandra was always there to encourage me, telling me not to worry and that things would be alright. Steven would make the coffee, Sandra would make the soup and we'd all discuss plans for the future: where we would live, how many children we would have, and of course business. Then we'd watch a film or sit in the garden.

I regularly thanked God for the blessing of the friendship I had with Steven and Sandra. I had many friends, but nothing like I had with these two crazy characters. To me, the friendship we shared was the stuff of lifelong friendships, and I could see the four of us rambling together through the countryside of many European countries when we were older and the children were grown up. Then going back home and eating noodle soup, drinking coffee and watching a movie.

I read many books on parenting. I hated Gina Ford's books and nicknamed her the Nazi woman. I knew that if my child wanted sleep, I would let them sleep. Without sleep, I am a bitch, no way was I going to inflict a lack of sleep on a child that would find processing huge amounts of information and finding a way to communicate with those around him. I read reports on health and diet during pregnancy, and chose to ignore most of it. Not eat peanuts, prawns and blue cheese? You are having a laugh! There was no way I would stop eating those things. My mother, her grandmother and thousands of other mothers around the world eat seafood, shellfish, and nuts and the children do not have the abundance of allergies that are inflicting the western world today, so bring on the jacket potato with prawn mayonnaise with a blue cheese and rocket salad! (Thankfully, the only allergy my boys have is hayfever and a little eczema, but that comes from their father's side.)

I continued to exercise daily, but as the bump got bigger cycling wasn't that comfortable, and I had gone from a steady run, to a jog to a walk and then a waddle. I was still on the treadmill a week before giving birth.

I had my first contraction about 10am the day before Khaalid arrived but thought it was just a twinge, so decided to go to aqua natal, then during the session, I had another one. It wasn't until after the session that a fellow mum realised what was going on. I wasn't a big eater, but that lunch time, I polished off a quarter pounder cheese burger and fries and then had apple pie and custard. She had spotted me in the pool having a contraction and then after lunch they were coming every 20 minutes. I still had to get to Foot Heaven on Ecclesall Road for a pedicure, and then home. This would take about an hour to do, so I estimated that I should only have three or maybe four more contractions, I would be fine. The ladies were not convinced but there was no way I was going into hospital without a pedicure. I hadn't been able to reach my toes for about a month, and I couldn't see me having time to give myself a pedicure for the foreseeable month, so I had to have that pedicure! Rana, a good friend's sister-in-law, just laughed at me when I told her what had happened, and gave me an extra special foot massage, it was blissful! She said I had to call her as soon as I got home, even though I was only five minutes from home anyway.

I gave her a ring as soon as I got home, and then called ramO at the office to let him know what had happened during the day. He wanted to come home straightaway. I told him that I was fine, I had the baby TENS machine, I was lying on the bed reading and that he should just finish his work off. I also told him that on his way home he should stop off at the shop and get me a big packet of hula hoops and a big slice of carrot cake. I hadn't had any cravings up until this point, but man did I want hula hoops and carrot cake!

The birth went really well, I was in labour for 16 hours, during which time I had plenty of gas and air. Actually ramO also had his fair share, the effects were similar to smoking weed, just much cleaner, but sadly only last while you are breathing it in.

I did end up having a shot of Diamorphine[5], which is not something I wanted, but this was maybe the only time I did listen to the doctor, after I had told ramO to phone his dad, my mum and his uncle who was also a doctor to check it was okay to have it.

The Diamorphine kicked in in no time and I lost 12 hours. The visuals were great to begin with, but then when I realised how much time I had lost, it scared me a little. It also gave me an understanding of why people who hate their life would take heroin based drugs. If you hate your life then this is a great way of just switching off and leaving the world. Not that I am recommending it, just sharing an insight that I gained. It was scary to think that anything could have happened during those 12 hours and I would not have known anything about it.

I do remember crying at one point shortly after I came back to my own version of normality; I thought I had wet myself. I was highly embarrassed until ramO and the nurse told me my waters had broke.

I was then taken into the water birthing room where I gave birth to Khaalid, after nearly pulling ramO into the pool with me during the contractions! When Khaalid came out I just wanted to hug him, I didn't care that he was covered in gunk, he was, and still is, perfect in every way. ramO and I both agreed that he looked like Gollum, all grey and slimy, bless him! I had never felt such love for a person and again this scared me. Could you love someone too much?

I remember lying on a beanbag after I had had a bath and Khaalid had been cleaned up. I was just staring at him; I couldn't take my eyes off him. The nurse finally snapped me out of it and asked if I wanted anything. I told her I wanted a cup of tea, milk, no sugar and some toast with butter and black pepper. I remember seeing her look at ramO and he laughed, "She always eats it, she's just weird." To which I chuckled and continued staring at Khaalid.

My next memory is being in the hospital bed and Khaalid is under my t-shirt resting on my chest. It was the most amazing feeling of closeness I have ever felt. He was so tiny and he fitted just perfectly. My family was complete for now, and in four years time, it would be complete forever when Khaalid's little brother came along. I always knew deep down I would have two boys; I had never imagined being a mother of girls.

Four days after he was born, we checked out of the hospital and went into Sheffield city centre to join the Pro Palestine march, an anti occupation demonstration. He was wrapped up warm, fast asleep and oblivious to what was going on. ramO and I both took it in turns to push the baby, ramO mentioning I had done enough pushing in the last few days.

It was a great day, and the coffee from Costa was so much better than the instant crap they served in the hospital! Life felt good. Life was good. I felt blessed and realised I was very blessed. I remember looking up to the sky and seeing a bright, yet cloudy day, and smiling. I was so thankful for God for everything he had blessed me with, and whispered a thank you to Him. ramO noticed my smile, gave me a hug and a tear escaped from my eye. I was immensely happy.

Being Khaalid's mother taught me so much about myself. It taught me what kind of person I wanted to be, what kind of life I wanted to give him, and how irrelevant material things are. The only thing that mattered to me was being with him. I became addicted to him. I couldn't think of anything but providing the best life, the best lessons and the best environments I could for him. I read everything to him, from marketing journals, how to succeed in business and of course the Mr Men books, Usborne Baby books and Dr Seuss. It didn't matter what I read to him, so long as it had a positive message and we were spending time together. We would visit the Botanical Gardens and have a picnic lunch, watch the squirrels, walk and look at the flowers. I walked for miles with him.

Our office became our second home. In one corner of the office we had a cot, changing mat and a mobile. Khaalid would lie in the cot asleep and when he was awake, he was held by either ramO or I while we worked. After a while, once he could sit up, we gave him his own keyboard to the side of ours so he could tap tap away. It wasn't plugged in of course but he loved it none the less.

After about seven months, I realised I couldn't keep him with us in the office anymore. He needed to be with other children so he could learn how to develop social skills with his peers. We were the first of our friends to have a baby, and had no family nearby for support. We had already decided and joined the nursery next door to the office and we really like one of the nursery nurses Claire. She became a good friend and babysitter to Khaalid, eventually becoming Aunty Claire. Khaalid thrived in the nursery and we eventually decided that instead of five half days, we would send him for three full days. The rest of the time he was with me.

When Khaalid wasn't with me I was still running the business and had started to mentor other people who wanted to be in business. I had been asked to do many public speaking engagements on business, work/life balance, how to be a great sales person and I loved it. I started to get more and more community work opportunities and realised that this was the kind of work I really enjoyed. It fitted in better with Khaalid's nursery times and I could always write the speeches whilst my prince was sleeping.

I took on an office manager and this enabled me to spend more time away from the office. ramO started to work overseas on client projects for long periods of time and came home every second weekend. It was hard, but the bond between Khaalid and I grew even stronger because of it.

I became involved with different ethnic communities to help develop their businesses. I got involved with schools and the Enterprise projects. I was asked to speak at seminars for the Sheffield Hallam University Enterprise Centre, Business Link, Yorkshire Forward and many more national and international business and community organisations. I was asked to take part in local and national Radio programmes for the BBC and independent stations. It seemed too good to be true.

Before I knew it, we were looking for schools. I knew which schools I didn't want, but there was one school in particular that we had done business with which I did want. I loved it. It was a great school; still is.

Once we had gone through the application process and been accepted, I had the difficult task of telling my mum that her only grandson was going to a private boys school. Our relationship was still not great, although she had been to visit us once a year since Khaalid was born. I was not looking forward to it. All my life for as long as I could remember, I had heard her say, "Don't get ideas above your station," and I knew it would reignite the sayings, "You think you are better than us," and would indeed lead to the question, "What's wrong with a state school?"

The truth was I wanted the best for my child, the best that we could afford without making life unbearably difficult for us all. One of the quotes that I have always loved was, "I never let my schooling interfere with my education," and I knew that at Birkdale, Khaalid wouldn't just be getting 'schooling' with books. He would be getting opportunities to travel, be part of a community that encouraged differences in faith, cultures and beliefs. The school was an enterprising school, a charitable school and it was also within a 10-minute car journey or 30-minute walk for us all. He would have the best of the book based education as well as a worldly education, all within easy reach. For us it was the best solution, but I knew all my family would think about is the fact that it was a private school.

Some of the parents at the nursery where Khaalid had attended were also rather put out at our choice of school. One parent even went on to ask how we could afford it. Quite simply – none of your business! But had we spent as much on cars, designer clothes and getting drunk at the weekend on champagne as she did, then maybe we would have struggled to pay for it. Who knows, but it was interesting how people were suddenly very keen to know how much money we had. How rude!

Shortly before Khaalid started at school, ramO was working in Luxembourg, one of the latest in a string of European locations. Khaalid was at nursery school, or rather at work as he described it, and I was at a business meeting at the Sheffield United Football Ground.

I remember standing with two friends Tim and Faris with a cup of coffee in my hand. We had been chatting about the presentation Simon Woodroffe, founder of Yo Sushi and the Yo! brand had just given us all. I went to have a sip of my coffee and all of a sudden started to feel sick. In that moment, I knew I was pregnant. When Tim asked me if I was okay, I simply replied, "Yes, I think I am pregnant – no – I know I am." I know it wasn't the answer he expected by the look on his face but the smile on both their faces made me laugh.

We sat down and Simon Woodroffe came and sat beside me. It was a very surreal moment. Here I was with a really inspiring man, who had a similar hedonistic past prior to business, and who had just made me laugh, having a conversation. He told me that he loved seeing me in the audience because I had a happy face and he knew I had understood some of his 'code' words and tongue-in-cheek humour.

We continued to speak about what I did and what he was up to next and then he was whisked away by the event organisers. Upon leaving, he told me to keep smiling my lovely smile, shook my hand and said, "Catch you later." I hope one day I will catch him later. He is a very cool guy.

Later that evening when I was telling ramO about the event, I told him that I was pregnant. He was excited, and yet he didn't believe it, and said he wouldn't believe it until he saw the blue line on the pregnancy test. He asked me how many I had done. When I told him none, I had just gone off coffee, he laughed again. He told me that I had to get two tests to bring with me to Luxembourg that weekend. I said, "Okay, but I know I'm pregnant."

Later that night Khaalid and I spoke about him having a baby brother or sister and he told me that he wanted a baby brother first and then a baby sister. I said we will just have to wait and see what God has in store for us, to which he replied, "Well, He is going to give me a brother first so I can wrestle with him like I do Baabaa⁶." Okay then, who am I to argue?

That weekend, Khaalid and I boarded the plane to Luxembourg, Khaalid's 15th or 16th time on an aeroplane already, and we were so excited to see ramO. Khaalid asked me if I had my 'wee wee sticks' with me and I said, "Yes prince, I do."

To which he replied, "Good Mummy, because Baabaa wants to know if I am having a baby brother or sister." He was so cute about it and I knew he would be an amazing big brother.

Upon arriving in Luxembourg the first thing I did was get the 'wee wee stick' out and do the test. I handed it to my boys and went to lie down, hands on my belly. I was already protective of this little angel growing inside of me. ramO was so excited and just kept chuckling to himself at how sure of myself I was. He asked me what I would do, if I wasn't pregnant. When I told him it doesn't matter, because I know I am, he just gave me the biggest hug, it was magical. Watching my boys sitting there looking at the 'wee wee stick' together is one of my happiest memories. Seeing their faces change from the concentrated looks into the big smiles was wonderful. Yet another gift from God.

Khaalid came running over to where I was lying down and kissed my belly and lay down next to me. I was so happy I had tears falling from the corner of my eyes. We all embraced as a family and lay down chatting for ages. It was beautiful. Khaalid was already thinking of all the things they could play together and the places we could go and then declared that he was going to be a big brother with a big smile on his face. At that point, we all got up, took a family photo and had dinner together. It was a wonderful evening.

That weekend was also the start of the World Cup in Germany, and because we were so close, we all decided to get on a train and go to watch England's opening game. We sat by the riverside and watch the match with all the others that had made it to Germany but couldn't, or didn't, get tickets. One man painted Khaalid with the Red, Black and Yellow face paint of the German flag and gave him the 'instant flag' face paint. I was dressed in a white jacket, red headscarf and my blue jeans, and ramO was in his jeans and t-shirt. Here we were in Germany as a couple with people looking at us, no doubt wondering what team we were supporting, but it made me smile because we were an international family that broke down stereotypes and confused those that only thought one way. It was great.

Khaalid fell asleep as the whistle blew for kick off. It was an okay game, the weather was good, the crowd okay, although some were rather unsavoury. I thanked God that he had been asleep[7]! As soon as the final whistle went, Khaalid woke up and asked when the football was starting. When we told him he had missed it he simply said, "Oh, but I wanted to see it. Can we watch it again?" ramO explained that it was over; put Khaalid on his shoulders and we went back to the hotel. I was really tired and decided to have a lie down whilst the boys went to have a kick about in the park of Bad Homburg.

I was very tired for the rest of the trip and put it down to the early stages of pregnancy and the travelling that we had just done. Okay so I wasn't driving, but I had travelled from Sheffield to Luxembourg to Germany back to Luxembourg and then to Sheffield, all whilst sightseeing in both Germany and Luxembourg. I continued to be tired for much of the pregnancy with our second child. I didn't get on well with my new midwife, not like I had with the previous midwife Sarah. This new midwife came across as very dismissive. She didn't like how I knew what kind of birth I wanted, how I confronted her stereotype of Muslim women. She didn't think it was right my husband 'was just leaving me to deal with everything by myself' even though I had explained to her that he wasn't 'just leaving me to deal with everything by myself'.

She had issues with the fact that I was still running a business, even though it was pretty much running itself at this point. We had started to outsource most of the work; we had machines that ran nonstop to keep orders ticking over. Our home was five minutes from our office and I had a home office set up so was in regular contact if anything needed doing. I had also been selling off a lot of stock because I wanted to take the business in a different direction. I had started to outsource many of the larger jobs to another reputable firm in the city and I was happy with the way things were going. I was still doing a lot of seminars and public speaking events and I was also in my fourth year as a member of the Sheffield Chamber of Commerce BME board. Life was good. Most of the work I was involved in was simply reading reports, making suggestions, writing bids or speeches and attending monthly meetings. I was working, all-in-all, maybe two weeks a month, four to five hours a day, spread out over the month. It suited my life. Most of the reading and writing was done whilst Khaalid was sleeping, and took my mind off missing my husband, who I spoke with maybe six to seven times a day.

Even though I had informed the midwife, she still felt it was all too much for me. When I told her that it may have been too much for her to do, it was for me something I loved doing and if I hadn't been reading and writing these business materials, I would be reading and writing other things. I simply decided this woman just had issues with anything that challenged her. Needless to say, we didn't get on, but with a shortage of midwives, I couldn't change to another one.

So I decided to make a call to the only straight talking Muslim sister I had a number for that I knew would give me the answers I needed to hear without sympathy, not the one I wanted to hear. It would be one busy woman to another and that sister was Ameena Blake, 'star' of the documentary 'Mum, I'm a Muslim' and head sister of the Muslim Association of Britain in Sheffield. Ameena and I didn't agree on a lot of things but we had a deep understanding and had a kindred spirit between us that held us tightly together in the sisterhood of Islaam.

But instead of hearing Ameena's voice, I heard another voice. A voice that would lift my heart for many years to come, and that voice belonged to one of the most inspiring women I had ever met, Dr Alison Buxton (Ali), mother of one, pregnant with another just like me and also a lover of coffee and open green spaces. We met the next day and my life has never been the same again.

---

1. Off the record' advice from one of the consultants while ramO was in hospital!
2. Just to clarify, I mean the contraceptive pills folks not the fun party ones!
3. How very British of me dumping the cause of my pain in Australia!
4. ramO told me the following piece of continental wit after working for a year in Luxembourg:
   A person that speaks three languages is trilingual ... a person that speaks two languages is bilingual ... a person that speaks one language is English!
5. The nice, media-friendly medical term for Heroin!
6. Baabaa is Daddy in Arabic, for those of you who were wondering.
7. One English supporter a few rows down felt it necessary to flash her boobs and Union Jack knickers at passersby every so often!

THIRTEEN

THE GREAT BIG UMMAH

Ali was a breath of fresh air and I loved her instantly. She was funny, generous and had the kindest soul. After we had shared stories and coffee, she started to tell me about this study circle that she went to, and it turned out to be the same study circle that Ameena had once told me about, one that I had reservations about going to because of the dire experience of the first one.

The first one had been a total nightmare for me. To be honest, I don't remember how I ended up there, or my first Muslim encounter in Sheffield. I do remember meeting a sister called Jamiila and then Ameena; I hit it off instantly with them. Jamiila called me Fajr, and she is still the only one to this day I allow to call me that. She was so lovely, and I think it was her that introduced me to Ameena. How I met Jamiila though is long forgotten because it feels as if I have always known her. I remember her being at a study circle up near an area of Sheffield I had never been to before called Wincobank. It had some amazing views across the city, and I remember nearly crashing the car because I was so distracted! Sheffield really does have some large hills! Once inside the centre, I remember sitting around a large table with other reverts, listening to them talk, hearing how they spoke with their children and thinking, *I don't want to be here*. The floor was dirty, the building was run down, and I thanked God that Jamiila's friendly face was there to send me smiles.

It felt strange being there; for many reasons. I had nothing in common with the sisters that were there other than the fact that we called ourselves Muslims, but listening to their thoughts and ideas on what it was to be a Muslim was so different to my own understanding. I had read that to work is an act of worship, but here were several females who didn't want to work, had no intention of working and were quite happy claiming the dole each week. When I mentioned that this was similar to gambling, which in Islaam is forbidden, they couldn't see the link. When I explained that gambling is forbidden because you haven't earned it and it is by chance you get the money, and being on the dole is by chance that you were born in the UK and you haven't earned the money, it still landed on deaf ears. I couldn't deal with the fact that another sister called her children, and the other children present 'brats'. I just wanted to cover Khaalid's ears to stop this negative environment seeping into his body. He was sound asleep though in his little car seat, and I thank God that he wasn't old enough to understand what was going on around us.

I remember going home and having a hot shower to make myself clean, and then soaking in a hot bath. I cried that night. But I returned because I thought maybe it was my prejudices, my ignorances. We are all born into circumstances that we cannot control and we make the best out of them. But week after week, I wasn't learning anything new about Islaam, I wasn't allowed to question in this environment, and the questions I was asking were far too deep for the sisters in the room. Jamiila said to me one day that the sisters in the room were still at the beginning of their journey and I was on a different journey; and not to worry about anything. I decided that she was right, we were on a different journey, and the journey they were on was not going to lead me to where I wanted to be.

After having spent a lovely day with Ali, she told me that she would ask her friend Rosie to collect me the next day as she was having a get together at her home. She told me I needed to get out and meet others and get a grip on things. So I waited the next day for Rosie to turn up and yet another amazing sister popped up in my life. Rosie was the house[1] version of me with her great taste in clothes and the ability to look great in everything she wore; she's the kind of person that would make a potato sack look fabulous! Rosie even knew of Diehard, the rave club I went to every Friday back in the day, as she had lived in Leicester. We did not stop talking for one second. We laughed and it felt so right to be in her company. She was a crazy girl and I knew I had found another great friend. We both loved fashion, although Rosie a lot more than me. She would make a bin bag look good by 'just throwing things together'. She was one of the funniest people I had met in a long time, and she also said what she thought. I just couldn't wait to tell ramO all about her.

Arriving at Ali's I was faced with about 10 other sisters, all as lovely as Ali said they would be. I remember sitting on a chair in her living room and looking at all these sisters. I let out a huge sigh of relief. This felt right. This felt like home, and for the next three years it pretty much was. Ali and I spent so much time together from that day on I had to keep pinching myself to make sure it was all happening. How on earth did all this happen so quickly? After all this time of wanting just one friend who 'got me' on pretty much every level, here I was with a group of girls that were in a similar situation to me, western reverts, who enjoyed learning, reading, family, cooking, music and nature, the simple things in life. One of the added bonuses was the discussions about everything and anything. We put the world to rights, discussed the trials and tribulations of motherhood, and we discussed the state of the Muslim world at large, the 'Ummah'.

I started to go to the new study circle with Ali and the sisters I had met at her home, and it felt good for a while. I know for some the thought of going to a religion study group smacks of some kind of religious extremism, but trust me this new study circle was more about how to just deal with life as a mother and a wife with Islaamic knowledge thrown in. We weren't planning on blowing up anything other than balloons. We weren't into making bombs just pots of coffee. I was finally surrounded by other women that shared so many of the same loves and wants in life. They wanted to learn about Islaam and think about it, not just accept everything that was said to them. These women were thinking women and for me this made all the difference.

Ali has a much more relaxed view of things and always laughs at me when I get off on one. I just can't help but get frustrated by the actions of so many Muslims. Some of the things they do have no logic and they certainly do not present Islaam in a good way. For me the bigger picture is simple. If we do not want people to think of Islaam as some antiquated religion that stinks of tribalism and backward thinking, or to be fearful of Islaam and Muslims, we have to behave in ways that alleviate those fears and concerns. It is not our job to preach at every given moment to every person. God doesn't need our help converting people, but the people need reassuring they are not living near a bunch of lunatics, people that think they are going to hell just because they do not believe the same things we do. I am a Muslim and time after time I am left speechless at some of the things I see and hear. Some of them are immensely funny, some of them just plain ridiculous. Others are just old cultural traditions that have been intertwined with faith over the centuries. If I get frustrated and angry, then is there any wonder there is so much Islaamophobia in the western world these days, something that is even entering the eastern world.

Some of the things that have driven me potty are things such as saying Salaam alaikum[2] as you pass from one room in your home to another when you are by yourself or with family… is it really necessary? You haven't left your home, you haven't been asleep for hours, all you've done is step from the kitchen into the dining room… or am I missing the point here? Where in the Qur'aan does it say I have to give Salaam to the furniture as I walk around my home cleaning? It doesn't, so I don't! If there is no proof, then I am not interested thank you very much. When I first said this to Ali, she just giggled at me and told me they are not giving salaam to the furniture. Some people believe it helps get rid of evil spirits that enter the home. That explanation didn't seem logical either, after all these spirits can't be that evil if they can be scared off by a few words! But hey, what do I know?

Ali and the girls got used to me having a rant on various subjects: segregation, being one of them. I firmly believe this is a cultural practice, simply because, if God wanted us to be segregated He would not have advised us how to behave in public in the Qur'aan, such as lowering our gaze. We are informed we are to be modest in our actions and how we dress. If we had to be segregated there would be two Ka'bahs in the holiest of places for the holiest of occasions – Hajj.

I remember being invited to a 3eed party where boys over seven years of age were not allowed so the sisters could take off their scarves. Seven years old! Seriously? Does a seven-year-old boy know about his sexuality and get sexually aroused around his mother and her friends when their scarves are not covering their heads? What on earth are their mothers teaching them? What kind of environment are these boys growing up in? Most 10-year-old boys I know are into Spiderman and Ben 10 and pretending to save the world, not get his rocks off during a 3eed party with his mum and her friends. Until a boy is able to have children, or is aware of his own sexuality it is not necessary for women to cover in his presence, and this doesn't happen until his voice begins to drop and hair starts appearing on his body. How many seven-year-old boys do you know with a deep voice and a goatee beard? I know of none, and really think some of these sisters need their heads looked at. But what do I know, hey? Bugger all it seems, obviously!

I would attend events put on by various different Muslim organisations, and I would always be a little disappointed with the amount of reverts that would be dressed in the traditional Arabic gown or Pakistani Shalwar Kameez[3]. I had nothing against people wearing them, but what I had an issue with is they were encouraged to wear it 'to be modest'. They would be told that to dress in a western way is immodest. For me this is wrong and causes more problems for reverts than necessary, especially for family members who may be worried about the conversion. It has caused estrangement for so many families, and the loss of the family members has proven too much for some. Many times I would have a phone call, or I would be taken to one side by a sister and asked why I still wore western clothes, why I hadn't changed my name. They asked me so many questions and the more I answered them, the more they opened up to me, many informing me they were thinking of leaving Islaam because it just didn't feel right anymore.

One young girl became a good friend of mine and yet she would never come to one of my many get-togethers because she just didn't want to face the 'rest of them'. I would reassure her that if anyone criticised her in my home, they would be asked to leave. Although she knew this to be true, she decided it was best to stay away and find her own way in Islaam, something I totally understood having spent the earlier informative years of my journey into Islaam by myself. When I think back now, I am so glad I had the opportunity to find things out without the sisterhood for two reasons. The first reason being I was able to sort out many of the cultural practices from Islaam and the second reason being the gift of friendship and sisterhood I received much later from Ali and Rosie was so much sweeter. Speaking of being sweet, another one of the sisters I met through Ali was the lovely Debbie. A fellow Michael Jackson fan and a lover of cake, at any time! Debbie introduced me to a world of cake without guilt so much so that the first time we ate cake together, our other fabulous girlie Monique couldn't stop laughing as we devoured half of a Chicago Town Double Chocolate Fudge Cake each! It was good, so good. Thankfully we didn't go halves all the time, but we did have weekly cups of tea and slices of cake over a good natter for hours. I know if it hadn't been for Debbie the birth of my second son may have proved fatal. I was told to go to the hospital as soon as possible, but with Jessop's Maternity Hospital being just beside the Severn Road Mosque in Sheffield, and it being the first day of 3eed, I was intent on going to pray with the sisters first. Under Debbie's strict supervision, and you don't argue with Debbie when she is telling you off, I missed 3eed prayers and as soon as I walked into the hospital and told them who I was, I was rushed into a ward and hooked up with wires, drips and heart monitors, I knew Debbie was right… she usually was.

I knew all along during the pregnancy that something was wrong. I knew my body and the way I was feeling wasn't just because 'I had a lot on' as my midwife kept telling me. I was feeling faint and dizzy for most of it. I was in a lot of pain. I was unmotivated, which for me was a big thing. I normally have so much energy, if I could bottle it and sell it, I would be a multi-millionaire overnight. I love cooking, but couldn't even be bothered to make cheese on toast. I love playing with Khaalid, but I couldn't even muster the energy to take him to the park for him to play. My feet were swelling up, I felt sick most of the time, and I even bled a few times. I had been for urine tests and diabetes checks, both came back with un-normally high levels, but none of these symptoms were put together. I found it extremely hard to breathe some times; I just wanted to sleep all day and night. Even though I kept informing my midwife of how I was feeling, she just wasn't interested.

The nursery team at Kids Unlimited were more supportive. They even stopped me from going home at one point after I had dropped Khaalid off one morning. They said I didn't look well and Claire, Helen and Emma T made sure I was kept under supervision in the staff room. They made me cups of tea and made sure someone was with me all the time. I will never forget what they did for me... even convincing the nursery manager Jo that me staying was the best idea.

When I left, I called my mum and asked her to come and stay with me for a few days because I was really scared something bad was going to happen. Unfortunately, we were going through another bad patch and when I asked her to come, she told me that she couldn't get time off work. I needed my mum, I told her I thought I might be losing the baby and it hurt me that she wouldn't take a few days off work to be with me. It was something I had gotten used to, mum being a workaholic and putting work first, but at a time like this I thought things would be different. The next day I felt worse than I had ever felt, so I called her again to beg her to come, but I couldn't get through at home. I called her work, only to be told by her boss that she had gone off on holiday for two weeks. I felt as though I had been hit by a 10-tonne lorry. I felt lost and alone. My mother had blatantly lied to me the day before by deceiving me – how could she?

As the days and weeks progressed, I got worse and worse. Khaalid was taken care of a great deal by Ali and Debbie when they could and the girls either came over and cooked, or collected us both to go to their home. Without them, I don't think I could have made it through.

ramO didn't know much about what was going on because I didn't tell him. I didn't want to worry him and have him cancel the contract he was working on. Luxembourg was a place he was enjoying, even though it was very quiet. He had made some nice friends there and the contract was a very nice one. And as the midwife kept telling me 'it's your second pregnancy – you have a lot on'. Maybe I did, maybe I just couldn't admit that to myself. Steven and Sandra were in Belgium at this point and so I couldn't pop over to see them in Nether Edge. I missed them terribly.

So I struggled on and then the night before 3eed hit me. It was the 22nd December, my sister's birthday. I remember speaking with her on the phone and then I lost my breath and couldn't get it back again. I thought my baby had kicked and winded me, but this was different. I just couldn't catch my breath at all. I said goodbye to Ellen, and as I put the phone down my other dear friend, Shaista, called. She could tell things were not good and told me to call the hospital, and if I didn't then she would come to Sheffield from the other side of Rotherham and 'batter me[4]' ... I phoned the hospital, I didn't want Shaista on my case! She was a tough one and even though sparks flew with us sometimes, she was another one that had melted the ice around my heart. I was not going to argue with her. I called the hospital and they told me they would send an ambulance. I told them I didn't need an ambulance and they insisted, so I told them my friend will bring me, I only live five minutes away. They gave me 30 minutes to get there. Debbie arrived in 15, my neighbour Cathy came around to sit for Khaalid.

Five minutes later, Debbie and I were at the hospital. We faced a long night, and I remember this really crap TV show being on. We answered so many of the questions correctly but still the presenter wouldn't listen to us... why would he? He couldn't hear us, we were not in the studio but the people who were... Oh my gosh! What muppets[5]! I'm sure they didn't have a brain cell between them... probably why it was on TV late at night, they didn't want to embarrass themselves on daytime TV!

Blood tests were taken and we waited for the results. Some came back okay but they were worried about the last results that had been sent for further analysis. We were told to wait, and me being me, worrying about Khaalid waking up and me not being there, I said I would go home and if there was a further problem they could call me. I only lived five minutes away. They insisted. I refused. They insisted. I refused. It went on for about 20 minutes and then I left. Cathy also had to get home and sleep as she was sick bless her, little did I know it was the initial signs of MND (Motor Neurone Disease).

The next morning the hospital called, I HAD to go back in, there was no question about it. I called Debbie, she was getting ready for 3eed prayers, so I said, "Well, let's go to prayers and then I'll go to the hospital."

This is when she put her foot down, "No Dawn, you ARE GOING to the hospital NOW!"

I don't remember much of my time in the hospital. I do remember waking up in a room, looking around and seeing no baby. I went to move and realised I couldn't. I was in an extraordinary amount of pain. I then deduced that maybe the baby had died.

I spent the next hour or so crying for the baby I had lost, when Khaalid and ramO came in smiling happily and Khaalid skipping around to the side of my bed saying, "I've just been to see my baby brother." I was confused. ramO told me that he was in the Special Care Baby Unit.

A memory that still haunts me today, was Naasir[6] crying in his incubator cot next to my bed and I couldn't stop him. I remember crying and feeling totally helpless. I had a drip hanging out of my arm, I could hardly move and all I could think of was shutting him up. I wanted to throw him against the wall. How could I? His own mother! As soon as the thought hit my head I fell back against the wall and dropped to the floor totally ashamed of myself. What kind of mother was I to think something like that? I didn't deserve to be a mother. That guilt would eat away at me for many years to come.

Another memory I have is a midwife telling me to get out of bed. When I told her I couldn't she simply replied, "If you wanted a cigarette you would." Having been a non-smoker for over a decade – well, of the cigarette variety anyway – I didn't see the relevance. I just turned my head and cried. How could she? Bitch.

The following few months are a complete blur. I don't remember anything else and have pieced together bits thanks to ramO, Ali, Debbie and Rosie. I thank God for them, daily.

When Naasir was about five months old, I revisited some of the study circles. Some of them I found enjoyable, but it got to a stage when I became frustrated again. I would want to clarify information and ask for proof from the Qur'aan, or simply offer an alternative viewpoint. When it was just a few of us, this would be fine, but when we had new people attending or when the more *conservative* members of the sisterhood arrived, I was not allowed to.

Now the trouble I had with this is simple. When I was younger I was not allowed to ask questions about God. I ended up finding out the answers for myself and that led to Islaam. Most new converts come to Islaam by thinking independently, but once they convert they are actively encouraged not to think independently. Only scholars are allowed to question and think. I found that every time I questioned hadeeth, Sunnah, and the teachings from those running the classes, they would be startled, and I would be accused of 'straying from the path' or 'being led astray by my own ego, passions, and desires'. When did the desire for truth and evidence become a bad thing? And surely this is what the purpose of reading and learning is all about, finding out the truth. When did being a sheep become an Islaamic way of being?

Having said all this over a slice of cake with Debbie, she would allow me to go off on one. So many would agree with me because, as Debbie says, "I bring common sense to the Ummah," whilst Monique would tell me I was a breath of fresh air to all the Dogma. We all know that in the Qur'aan, we're told not to follow our forefathers blindly and question our faith, and I stick firmly to this because the more we question the more we strengthen our faith.

So many new Muslims are scared of getting things wrong and many Muslim leaders take advantage of this. They prey on the fragility of the situation and bombard newcomers to the faith with horror stories of straying from the path and the dangers of mixing with the unbelievers, which includes many reverts' family members. I have seen with my own eyes how some of the leaders, who belong to some of the Muslim Associations in Britain, have told newcomers some cultural or tribal practices and the newcomer has believed them because, sadly, they do not know any better.

The 'leaders' are in such an important position, and yet so many do not know the difference between Islaam and cultural practices, even the wording they use within the study groups are cultural and not correct. Many new Muslims are given Urdu words, such as Qurbaani for the slaughter during Pilgrimage to Mecca, and told they are Islaamic words. This is incorrect and for this reason: If you are addressing the group only in Urdu because that is the common language, then by all means use an Urdu word. But if the common language between those attending is English, and you are teaching in English, then use English, as we're in England; then give the Arabic word, as the Qur'aan's in Arabic. The people teaching use Urdu words because they don't know any better. If they don't know they're using the incorrect term how can we trust the knowledge they are sharing is Islaamic not cultural? We can't. So we have to question, we have to check and we have to learn by ourselves in addition to what people tell us.

I know many of the study circle leaders love Islaam, and they want to help others. I know they want to share what they have learnt, but some have become so culturally blinded, forgetting some of the more important stuff. To dismiss me simply because I want proof and I want to question them, is not the way to go because if they are dismissing me and my questions, chances are they will dismiss others and their questions the further down the road they get, or the individuals will lose the ability to think for themselves and just start to repeat the rhetoric they have been told, simply because they want to be accepted. They do not want to be told they 'have lost their way' as I have been told on more than one occasion.

I came to realise with many of the Muslim groups and events that to question Sunnah and hadeeth leads to being ostracised and having people be warned about being with me. I remember walking out of the last study circle I attended and a couple of sisters coming outside after me to welcome me back into the group. When I said no and stated my reasons, I was greeted with the comment, "It is better to mix with bad Muslims, than to mix with good non-Muslims." It took me a moment to realise this sister was serious about what she was saying. I couldn't help but laugh at her because I would rather be with good non-Muslims than mix with bad Muslims any day!

Stepping away from the study circles and events was the best thing I could have done. I was so much happier now I wasn't being told I was not wearing the correct clothes in the correct way, or that plucking my eyebrows will send me to hell, not entering a room with the right foot, as opposed to the left foot, or saying a dua mini-prayer prior to going to the toilet, cooking a meal, going to sleep, blinking, moving… etc I hadn't realised how these things had been driving me insane!

Not hearing this Hadeeth or that Hadeeth every time to 'guide me on the correct path' was blissful simply because so many of them are a load of rubbish, and many more contradict the teachings in the Qur'aan. People spout them out of their mouths as if the Hadeeths were God's word. They are not, they are sayings and practices of the Prophet, and many I would say are taken totally out of context and value. I have been told not to eat with anything but my right hand because the Prophet only ate with his right hand. Well he also slept on a straw mattress and rode a camel or a horse. Are you going to sell your mattress and build yourself a stable to house your horse or camel? God created us with a brain and stated very clearly that Islaam was for all of time. So here's the thing. If we are thinking people, and Islaam is for all of time, then surely the new inventions we come up with and the more we develop our understanding of the world and our bodies, the more of a testament it is to the amazing creation that we are? Following all these Hadeeths and Sunnahs probably means I should have written this book with a feather on papyrus using the ink from squid!

With the help of Ali, a fellow foodie, I started to find out where I could buy 'proper halaal meat' from, even though the meat I had been buying from the Real Meat Company was killed in the same way, it just hadn't been blessed with 'in the name of God' at the time of slaughter, every other method, the throat slit, blood drained, no electrical stunning, was implemented. I spoke with Richard Guy who owns the Real Meat Company and he informed me of the way the animals were reared, slaughtered and the process after the slaughter had taken place and it was in line with the guidelines. Ameena, the sister most people in Sheffield turned to for advice on Islaamic matters, told me the meat was probably more halaal than the stuff in the 'halaal' butchers. I have to say I would agree, as the majority of the 'halaal' butchers in the Sheffield region are disgusting. There is so much cross-contamination I walked out of many never to return. There are no Health & Safety guidelines adhered to, and some of them I wouldn't keep pigs in! The problem the Health & Safety Executive has though is if they went and investigated the butchers shops, the community would cry 'Islaamophobia' and the press would be all over it. Simple truth is, if the shops were not so disgusting, and the basic food hygiene rules were implemented, then HSE wouldn't be visiting, would they? Clean up your act halaal butchers of Sheffield, and probably most of the UK, and realise that not every Muslim wants crappy meat. We also do not only want Pakistani style cuts. There are loads of Arab Muslims in the Sheffield area, many more reverts and a good steak, top side or silver side of beef wouldn't go amiss for Sunday lunch!

After a while, I started to become disillusioned with many Muslims I met. I realised that if I had met many of them before becoming a Muslim, I probably would not have looked so deeply into Islaam. Then I realised, if I allowed the behaviour of these Muslims to stop me from connecting with Islaam and the beauty of the Qur'aan, I was ignorant and stupid. Plain and simple.

I chose to stay in the company of Ali, Rosie, Debbie, and Monique, later on Amera, and Khadija popped up and my sisterhood was complete. Amera, Khadija, and I loved a drop of non-alcoholic wine with lunch as well as a large pot of coffee. Khadija was a Sheffield United fan and would attended many of the matches before coming over to mine for dinner. Gary, our big Geordie revert friend, would also often come over and eat with us, as well as wow his audiences on Facebook with his mock radio show Radio Hijri. Gary and ramO were much older than me and most of the songs they shared a love of I had no idea about. Many weekends our home would be filled with laughter until the early morning, after having spent the day in the garden by the bonfire, eating and playing with the boys.

Amera was becoming part of the furniture. She began spending a lot of time with me and the boys, either at our home or in the city centre, the Winter Gardens and Peace Gardens being our favourite spots. Our friendship became stronger every day. We shared secrets we didn't share with anyone else. Our friendship is one of total acceptance. I can be 100% of me with her, say and do things I know my other friends would disapprove of. If I wanted to have a spliff I know I could do that in her company and she would not look down on me, she would not say 'haraam' and tell me not to do it. If I felt I needed a break, she'd send me outside, but you see, I never really needed to. I had her, I had Ali and

Debbie. But when I did, it was okay to. I loved her even more for that, because I knew she totally accepted me, as I did her.

Another dear friend, Bernadette, would stop by for coffee unannounced which I loved. I realised that my life was full of wonderful people, Muslims and non-Muslims alike.

Rachel, a friend of mine for many years in the business sector became a very dear friend.

And with Steven and Sandra as friends too, I don't think I could have asked for a better group of friends.

That was until I met Asmaa and Teema, two very special sisters from Morocco. They blessed me with their gift of friendship in such a way that I sometimes felt overwhelmed. Asmaa and I would go walking at the weekend; we shared a friendship that blossomed from the beginnings of Teacher and Student. I taught Asmaa English and in return she taught me Arabic and I guess, more importantly, to relax more. Teema was the Qur'aan teacher for Ali, Debbie and the other sisters at Severn Road Mosque, but our friendship developed into something deeper than I had imagined it would. I learnt something about Teema that betrayed her sweet and innocent persona; she was a fellow activist and Women's Rights advocate. Finding this out made me giggle because I would never have guessed it with her sweet and innocent look and those long fluttery eyelashes of hers.

I had my friends, we studied and learnt about Islaam together and we accepted each other with a deep love and respect that I have never known elsewhere. My Muslim sisters and I had created our own special family, and it is one of the best things I have helped to create in my life. We no longer attended Islaamic events as most were more about integration issues to do with the Pakistani community and had little to do with Islaam. We no longer had to pray in a dirty room no bigger than a store room. Do these Imaams not know that men and women were equal in the eyes of God? Would they allow their mothers to pray in dirty broom cupboards? Sadly, some of the Muslim men I've met probably would! Even more sadly, many of the Muslim women I've met would allow themselves to!

I had become very happy and, although ramO was now working away in Europe frequently, I was not lonely. Never a day went by without seeing one of the sisters. The days my boys and I spent with Ali and her boys were some of the happiest days in my life. Sitting in her garden with a fresh pot of coffee, dinner cooking in the oven, whilst two little boys ran around pretending to be Indiana Jones, Ben 10 or Optimus Prime, whilst the other two slept peacefully, fills my heart with joy still to this day. What was also nice was we could just be. We could admit our faults without being condemned for them, not that Ali ever was, not sure how anyone could be upset with Ali to be honest with you. But I could never tell them I still had the odd spliff or two, not like I could Amera. But I guess you know now, hey girls? One of the most precious gifts Amera, Ali and Debbie's friendships was giving me was just accepting the fact that I shouldn't be hard on myself when I do get things wrong. I still found I was hard on myself when they were not around, and I knew I could be hard on others. I enjoyed admitting that I was wrong because it meant I was learning something new. Admitting my faults enabled the first step to resolving them, and sharing them with Ali, Debbie and Amera was a relief. I realised that I made things so much harder than they needed to be, and through my desire to have my mum become proud of me, I forgot that I only need God to be proud of me. I knew my friends would tell me to behave or get a grip on myself if I stepped over the mark and it was so nice knowing that I had such a wonderful group of friends and a husband who loved me, and it really did make such a difference. I started to celebrate all the simple things in life in a way I had never done before.

It helped that I was in the process of selling off all the assets of our businesses, and handing clients over to trusted competitors. I couldn't cope with my health problems and being a mother of two by myself, whilst ramO was working overseas. I also realised, lying in the hospital, that I didn't want to provide multimedia services for the rest of my life. I was also done writing marketing proposals and press releases. Letting go of the businesses allowed me to simply rejoice in life itself; focus on the new direction life was taking me in. I was able to let go of many things I had allowed to drag me down. Yes, I was immensely happy, but in an instant I could be deeply sad. I knew a lot of it stemmed from being poorly during the pregnancy with my second child, letting go of the business we had had for over a decade; yet even though I was very happy, my life was moving in a new direction with many things to be grateful for, new opportunities were coming up, I was deeply depressed.

I went through all the things in my life that I should be grateful for, and was grateful for. I had friends who viewed faith as very much a way of life. We all agreed that it is about being kind to others, taking care of family and friends, as well as myself. Something I was beginning to realise I wasn't doing very well. I knew faith was about being clean and tidy; helping out a neighbour or a stranger in a time of need, not killing someone or hurting others. I had all these in check. I knew that all religions share the belief that regardless of our faith, or non faith, that we should all be good and kind, respect ourselves, our parents and each other. Was I doing that? Respecting others? Yes. Respecting myself? Erm, not so much.

It was my other friend Beki, a self-confessed 'Jesus freak' of 10 years, that made me realise that I was not taking care of myself enough, not loving myself enough. Why though? I had everything I wanted and more besides. Why was I having such dark thoughts? What was missing?

One day Beki and I were chilling out in her flat discussing how we get this 'feeling' that we should be good, and how God made us that way. We went off on so many tangents and it didn't matter how much we discussed we always kept coming back to how all of these things we feel, experience, see, touch and taste leads to the belief that there is something much bigger than any of us can comprehend. God created us with these good morals, these feelings and the fear of what others may think of us, but at the end of the day we know that it is not our neighbours, friends, colleagues or other parents that we will meet on the Day of Judgement. We stand before our Creator, not Mr and Mrs Jones, which then made us crack up laughing because her parents were called Mr and Mrs Jones. It was funny at the time. One of those moments you had to be there for, really.

Living in Sheffield had been such a huge blessing for me. Having grown up in Friday Bridge, my world was now so different. I saw so many different people from around the world, heard so many different languages on a daily basis, and yet even with the international population and Sheffield being the fourth largest city in the UK, it still felt like a big village, something London and Oxford never had. I had gotten to know

Muslims from around the world and I truly believe that my faith deepened just because I lived in Sheffield and the people I came into contact with, not to mention seeing nature at its most impressive in the Peak District.

Seeing all the different traditions from so many different families made me realise even more than ever that I have to own my faith, because if I didn't, it could be diluted and lost. I had to have faith in my own faith and my own knowledge. I heard so many people tell me about this scholar and that scholar, but the thing with scholars is this: for every scholar that provides you with an opinion (and that is all it is an opinion) I could find a dozen more to disagree with that opinion. I started to learn about all these volumes of books that explained Islaam, again based on someone else's opinion and research. I started to consider why this other person's research and opinions were more important than mine were? I am the one that has to stand before God on the day of judgement, not even my mother can vouch for me or against me on that day, and yet I have to put my faith and fate in the hands of someone else? Call it trust issues if you like, and I'd probably agree with you, but who says these people are the ones that own my faith? Who says I should follow the word of a man who has only read things that confirm his knowledge? I have read so many books on so many different religions, books on science, evolution and history, books for and against religion and books on 'the human condition', surely the learning I have must count for something?

And here was the crux of my unhappiness; I didn't trust myself because I was in a situation I had never been in before. I had worked all my life; I had planned everything that I wanted to do, by when, from the age of 16. I had had my own business from age 21, now that was gone. I was a mother of two boys, and I got so caught up in the day-to-day life, that I had forgotten to plan. I was tired and exhausted more than I had ever been. I missed being with my best friend ramO. I missed my mum and dad, and my sister. I missed having a professional project. I was a housewife and mother and it scared me. Even though I knew being a great mother was more important than any other profession, I felt lost. Who was I now? What had I achieved? Had I met my goals for being a mother thus far?

Again, I faced Ali and she told me to get a grip once again, my eldest son was five, my youngest was still a baby, it was not time to start evaluating my skills as a mother or imparting deep wisdom on the boys just yet. I just had to enjoy life. Debbie told me to stop hiding and come over and eat cake. So I did.

On the way home from Debbie's I had a telephone call from a producer at Channel 4. Would I be interested in being in a documentary by them to dispel the false myths and perceptions of Muslims? You bet I would!

---

1. House music was dance music similar to techno, but tended to be calmer and attract a more stylish crowd!
2. Peace be upon you.
3. We think Shalwar Kameez comes from the Arabic words Sirwaal, the traditional word for something like trousers; and Qamees, the traditional Arabic shirt, similar to what would be called a 'granddad shirt' in the West.
4. Beat me up.
5. Idiots.
6. The name means "the one to bring about victory".

FOURTEEN

CHANNEL 4 & THE RACIST ATHEIST`

Sometimes I agree to do things without thinking them through properly. Taking part in this documentary with Channel 4 was one of those things. I was approached by a Channel 4 producer during the springtime of 2007, following a recommendation made by our friend Reem. At the time she was editor of the only Arab British magazine printed in English. ramO had a regular feature in the magazine and so Reem and I had met on several occasions, sharing many frustrations about the state of Muslims in Britain. I knew that I was fed up with seeing meek and mild, 'born' Muslims of Eastern origin, especially South Asian, representing 'Muslims in the UK'. I was a Muslim in the UK. I had in fact grown up all my life in the UK; lived and socialised in many of the subcultures that make up the diversity among the 'English English'. I was also fed up with many of these Muslims representing me when they sounded as though they had 'just got off the boat'. I also knew I wasn't the only one who felt this way. I also knew that when these Muslims appeared on TV, that was when most of the people that were fuelled with hatred towards Islaam just had their narrow-minded, ignorant and xenophobic views confirmed. These brown-faced 'Muslamics¹' had no idea about what it was to be English, and knew so little about the subcultures of English life, so they had no way of relating to the larger non-Muslim community. I thought to myself, *Thank God that I have been given this opportunity to put across a different point of view, someone that many in the UK could relate to.*

Having met the production team (Laura, Howard and Christian) I trusted they, as editors of the show, would do a good job after the many reassurances by Christian and Howard that this documentary series was to 'dispelled the myths and change the attitudes towards Muslims in the UK'. I put my faith in them and we set to work.

The first day we met the participants was daunting. Not only had I only been out of bed about a month after the serious life threatening illness with my second pregnancy, but I was also still breast feeding. I was not very confident in the way I looked as I had gained a huge amount of weight during the pregnancy due to the illness. The lack of exercise over the last four months had turned most of the muscle I had gained due to daily weights and cardio work into fat. I was not at my best physically, emotionally or mentally, but I was not about to pass up this opportunity just because I didn't look good or because I was scared of leaking breast milk on my outfits! I was also aware that some of the participants were racist, atheist, or 'die-hard Christian'. Debating is a strong skill of mine, but just how much of it were we going to be doing? How much of the information that I had to share, after having decided to become a Muslim 15 years earlier, would I be allowed to share and how much of it would the participants be willing to take on board? How much were the Imaams and 'scholars[2]' going to listen to what I had to say, but also how much were we mentors going to listen to the participants? How much of what they had experienced would we listen to? How many myths that they had floating about in their heads were they willing to let go of? Were we all about to enter a no holds barred ring of religious fighting or would we, as I hoped and prayed, be able to build bridges and connect on different levels, putting our religious differences aside?

Walking through the archway into the cafe area where the participants were sat waiting was interesting for me as I looked at the other mentors.

We had Suleiman who was of Pakistani decent, had lived in South Africa but now lived in London. I remember the first time I met him I couldn't help but giggle to myself. Here was a man in what looked like a black Bruce Lee outfit, with trousers far too short[3] topped off with a black 'Puffa' jacket that wouldn't look out of place in the Jungle[4] room. He wouldn't look at me during the meeting, and it took him a while to talk directly to me, but that was his way of showing me respect, and I respected him for it.

We then had Mohammad, a Nigerian who had lived part of his life in Brixton as part of the black Muslim community. He was dressed in his white Galabiyya[5], with his red and white Kuffiyya[6] tied around his neck, his little white 'Muslim' hat,[7] and his plastic carrier bag, which would provide many moments of comedy throughout the next few weeks, not to mention a pain in the film crew's backside.

Ajmal Masroor was the lead mentor and was one of the key players in how the show would be edited, so I was told. I had done my research on him and found out he was in the running to be the Liberal Democrats candidate for Mayor of London. He was also a key player in the Muslim Society of Britain, one of the many Muslim organisations in the UK, and the only one that held events that sounded interesting and inviting, such as the Living Islaam Camp held every two years. Friends of mine knew of him and shared some YouTube links with me. He sounded liberal enough, and we shared similar views.

Then there was me. The only woman, the only white face, the only one who wasn't a 'scholar' and the only revert. A little giggle escaped me when I pictured the faces of the participants.

I had been told that there was a glamour[8] model called Kerry; the Birch family, comprising two daughters and a son with mother and father; Carla and Ash – Carla was a 'devout' Christian and Ash was a 'lapsed[9]' Muslim. His family didn't like her and she was doing this documentary to 'learn more'; we had Phil the racist, atheist, illiterate, taxi driver; Hayley who was interested in lots of different spiritual ways of being; Luke the cross-dressing gay who was interested in learning more.

I knew who was who in about five seconds. I could tell Luke would be fun. I knew Hayley was there to learn but I sensed that Carla was there to just attack, along with Kerry, Phil and Mrs Birch. Mr Birch was genuinely interested in the process and wanted to help widen his children's view of the world, after all living in Harrogate, the whitest, most middle class small town in England was not going to offer them diversity of any kind.

I felt the hatred from Phil the first moment we looked at each other. He didn't like me and as the show progressed I found out why. He called me a traitor to my country, accused me of being brainwashed and shouted me down at every opportunity when I was attempting to answer his questions. Nothing that hadn't been said or done to me before, but his words came with such venom he deeply upset and frightened me.

Our first 'family outing' was to a mosque in Bradford. I couldn't believe it. I thought we were supposed to be dispelling the myths and stereotypes, not reinforcing them! I was really angry about this and told Claire, the other producer, that this was a big mistake. All this would do is confirm and heighten the prejudices. I wasn't far off either. The Imaam of the mosque didn't even want to allow us to give the participants a copy of Muhammad Asad's translation[10] of the Qur'aan and his story The Road to Mecca, a story about his conversion to Islaam. The Imam caused a number of problems, which delayed the filming for over an hour. A typical response from someone who wanted to give himself more prestige and power than he actually had. During this visit to the mosque, I had to show the women how to perform the ritual cleanse of Wudu. Whilst doing this, Mrs Birch, Kerry and Carla took great pleasure in making fun of the whole process; a great example for a mother to be setting her child: make fun of those that do not share your views or traditions, even if they are doing their best to help you. What the three of them failed to realise was, I did share many of their traditions and I'd lived with their racist and prejudiced views for the first 18 years of my life, and continued to hear those views every time I went home to the village I grew up in. So much for them wanting to learn more and teach their children about diversity! Their mocking caused more delays, delays I could do without. I needed to express[11] the build up of milk and the more they delayed the more pain I was in.

Whilst I was attempting to show the females participants how to pray, the mocking continued and was very off-putting. I wanted to tell them, "Shut the fuck up and have some manners," but where would that leave us all? The milk building up in my breasts was becoming more and more painful every time I leant forward in prostration. The breast pump had been left back in Harrogate, and had we not had the delays caused by the Imaam, Mrs Birch, Kerry, and Carla, we would have been back in time for me to express. They were not my favourite people because now I had to express in the mosque by hand, wasting milk that God had blessed my child with… Haraam! And I had no spare clothing with me!

In the cars to and from the different locations, both the mentors and the participants were placed together. I remember wondering if the participants would use this time and ask questions about why I had chosen to become a Muslim, how my family had reacted and other such questions that I had been bombarded with over the last five years since I had started covering. I wondered how many assumptions they were making about me, and the other mentors, but also how many assumptions we, the mentors, we making about them and their lifestyles. I had met many people in my life from drug dealers in my raving days and prostitutes through some of the community work I had done. Many had been forced down this route as young as nine and ten by their parents and it was through the community groups that they were seeing there was another way. I wondered what had made Kerry become a glamour model. I wondered why Phil was so aggressive towards me, more so than the other mentors. To be honest, Phil gave me the creeps and reminded me of the ghost in the film *Ghost* that teaches Sam, AKA Patrick Swayze, to move things through anger. I remember thinking this on one of the many journeys we had and giggling to myself because I remembered the hardcore track that includes the line, "You've got to feel all your anger, all your pain and push it way down into the pit of your stomach and let it explode like a reactor!" What an excellent tune!

During the first week the mentors were teamed up, Mohammad and Suleiman together, with Ajmal and I together. We were to visit the participant's homes and remove 'contraband items'. This was really difficult for me to do. I felt so rude and like some kind of Naziesque inspector. Who was I to tell these people the things they had in their home were inappropriate? But then again, they had signed up to the process and so had I.

The first home we visited was Kerry's. She had done her best to present her front room as best she could, and she had 'cleaned' her kitchen, but what I saw when I opened the fridge made me wretch my stomach. I had to step back and let Ajmal take the lead. The insides of the fridge were filthy and as we walked upstairs I began to realise that cleaning and taking care of her children were not the top of her list. Whilst she had spent several thousand pounds for breast enlargement, she had failed to provide a clean and safe bedroom for her two children. It took all my willpower not to cry at the state of their bedrooms. I had never seen anything like it, and the mother in me just wanted to sweep them up in my arms, take them to the nearest B&Q and ask them to choose a wallpaper they liked, some shelves and then visit Dunelm and get them some fresh bedding. It wouldn't cost much but it would make a huge difference to the rooms and hopefully to their lives. They would have a little space of their own, for their age. It didn't end there either. There were endless amounts of pornographic magazines just stacked about, with images so vulgar that I wondered how these two innocent little minds had interpreted what they saw. Then we saw Kerry's son's video games collection. He was not very old, maybe six or seven and he was playing 18+ games. I was shocked at some of the titles and couldn't believe any mother who loved her child would allow such a thing. It made me think about so many of the things I had witnessed in my life. I thought about so many of the children in the community groups that I had worked with and how we as parents mould our children. I began to question how things had got to a point that parents were so blinded to the damage they were doing by allowing pornographic images to be seen by children so young. Why did Kerry think it was okay to spend money on her breasts but not put carpets, curtains, and clean bedding in her children's bedrooms? Was it Kerry's parents' fault she did not know how to raise a child? Was it their parents' fault? But then I kept coming back to the adage that my grandmother and mother had taught me, "It takes a community to raise children," and in the end I didn't feel angry with Kerry, I just felt sorry for her. I had never felt pity for anyone and it was a strange feeling to have. I was asked and filmed by Laura how I felt about the experience after we left. I am not sure what I said now but I know it wasn't included in the end product. Probably just as well. I remained silent on the way to Luke's house contemplating what I had just witnessed, felt and experienced. This process was a bigger learning curve than I had ever anticipated and I was grateful more now than I had been, for being asked to take part. I was learning a lot even if the participants weren't.

As we arrived at Luke's house, I took a deep breath and he welcomed us into his home in his usual cheery fashion. I had already come to like Luke a lot and when we started going through his music collection for contraband items, I found so many of the same CDs that I still listened to. How could I get rid of his CDs when I had the same ones in my home? I mentioned this to Ajmal and said that if the items were to be removed, he had to do it, because I wouldn't remove them. We were then faced with the kitchen and memories of Kerry's kitchen flooded my mind, but I needn't have worried. Luke's kitchen was as clean and tidy as I had hoped a gay man's kitchen would be. The only 'dirty' part was the dog's litter tray. Again, I didn't want to remove the dog from the home altogether, but Luke had already found his pooch a holiday home for the process. In fact, Luke was really into the process of learning. He had even phoned up his local kebab shop to find out if the kebab meat had pig in it. When we opened Luke's freezer we found a bottle of Absolute Vodka. Luke asked me if I had ever drank alcohol. My answer, "Like you wouldn't believe, but Vodka only passed my lips in jellies or Vodka soaked melon balls. My favourite was Baileys, which I used instead of milk in fresh coffee, and the drinks of choice were Dry Martini and Lemonade or a Pimms and Lemonade. If we were talking straight up serious drinking then it was whiskey of the Bells or Jameson kind. Bells with two ice cubes and Jameson straight up!" I could see Luke was ever so slightly impressed and even more intrigued, which showed, as he and Hayley were the only ones to start asking me questions about the journey I had taken.

Ajmal was slightly taken aback that I knew what a bottle of Vodka looked liked, but having worked in the bar industry, I could tell him not only what the drink was if you showed me a part of bottle, if you asked me to name the region it was distilled in, I could have done that for you too. I knew alcohol, especially wine, ask my friend Russell. I impressed him after a night at Diehard when he pulled bottle after bottle of red wine out of his wine rack and questioned me on every bottle. Top marks to the girl skinning up on the couch! Unfortunately, we never did get around to the raving and the drugs I had taken, but I knew Luke suspected. There was no way he could not suspect from some of the knowing looks we shared regarding his clubbing escapades and music collection.

Several days later I was told to take Kerry shopping for the day to buy some clothes. Again I discovered we were off to the city nicknamed 'Bradistan[12]' for the shopping. Taking us to Bradford infuriated me even more. We were compounding the image that Islaam belonged to the South Asians, and that their clothing was the only clothing Muslims were allowed to wear. As we were also in a very traditional part of Bradford, I chose to wear my scarf in the traditional Arabic style out of respect to the local residents. As Kerry and I were talking I was informing her of the protection being covered up gave us from the sun; how it wasn't just to protect us from men who couldn't control themselves. I was also explaining how the niqaab[13] was pre-Islaam and mainly worn by men rather than women as they travelled across the deserts, and the only women to wear niqaab, which was mainly white, were the women in the Royal households if they have a disfigured face, like having a harelip for example[14]. Unfortunately the editing team did their very best during the editing process to cut out all the interesting bits and manipulated the things I said to make me look stupid. I was deeply upset with Ajmal, Dominic, and Christian about this and felt betrayed by them all. I wanted to take Kerry to some English high- street clothing stores like H&M or Primark where I knew she would be more comfortable, as even I don't buy clothes from South Asian shops! Trying to find something that fitted Kerry's likes and dislikes, as well as trying to accommodate those huge breasts of hers, was a difficult challenge. I didn't like most of the clothes and I could tell this was a really tough challenge for Kerry too. I actually felt really proud of her because this was one of the first times she really started asking questions and listening. It's just a shame it wasn't shown to the audiences on Channel 4.

The days spent away from Carla and Phil were blissful. I really did not enjoy being in their company. They were not in the process to learn, just to attack at every opportunity. Never once did Carla listen to the answer she was given. She started to turn discussions into racial attacks and several times I had to remind her that I was in fact English and if she could just see past the hijaab then we probably had more in common than either her or I would like to admit. We were both successful business women. We were both attempting to deal with a mother-in-law of a different culture, one of the hardest challenges I have ever faced, and continue to face even after 16 years of marriage. Having a moment to speak with Ash, her Pakistani British boyfriend was interesting. He was a Muslim by birth, and he believed in the concept of Islaam but by his own admission he did not practise. He enjoyed the trappings of a very liberal lifestyle and the temptations that were placed in front of him. I knew that both he and Carla were both partaking in things they had agreed not to take part in during the three week process. Having done similar things in my life, I had the knowledge and the experience to spot the aftermath that follows. I remember being in Carla's apartment and seeing her cross her body when she walked past a 'picture' of Jesus. When I looked at Ash, I asked him how he felt when he saw her do that. Respectfully, he said, "That's her choice in belief."

Looking at the picture together I said, "Don't you think he would look more like an Arab seeing as though he was born in Palestine, instead of having blonde hair and blue eyes? He looks more like the Greek God Zeus than anything."

I knew Ash was smart enough to know what I was saying, but I wondered if he would make the connection himself. Whilst I was on my journey of faith, I studied the symbolism of religious transfer over the centuries; it was a common occurrence to use familiar dates and imagery for the 'new' faith to manifest itself in its new followers.

Later that day Carla and I were to spend time together making a halaal meal – I chose to make chicken fajita, something not seen as 'Muslim food', as the production crew had chosen to compound the idea that Islaam belonged to South Asians in the country, by sending us all to Bradford and then sending Kerry and me off to a South Asian clothing store, forgetting that Islaam first came to the Arabs. A day out in London on Edgware Road would have been great! I could have taken them to some really great clothing stores and food shops, but alas Pakistan was winning in the Islaamic stakes, as well as in the cricket. Carla was surprised I was making South American food and had to ask, "How is this halaal?" When I told her egg, chips and beans were halaal the confusion on her face was amusing. She really had no idea, but then I couldn't blame her, neither did a lot of 'born' Muslims.

A distant friend once told me, "Asians are the best Muslims on the planet now, remembering to honour the code of Islaam!" Except many still believed it was okay to commit 'honour killings' and to preach tribalism. Some of my Pakistani friends are doing their best to combat the cultural tribalism by re-educating their parents, uncles and aunts and neighbours. But like Carla, Phil, Kerry, and Mrs Birch, their beliefs and prejudices were so deeply ingrained and based on ignorance, that it would take more than three weeks to overturn the beliefs of the participants and a lifetime to undo the beliefs of the older Pakistani mindset, especially with the extremists in the community.

During our cooking session I asked Carla what her plans were when she got married. She told me that she intended to give up work and be a full-time mummy. When I asked her why, she told me she wanted to spend time with her children teaching them, playing with them and just enjoying them. When I asked her why it was okay for her to make that choice but not for South Asian Muslim women[15], this seemed lost on her. Christian got it, and he realised she had completely missed the point I was making so asked for a re-run. We did the scene again and she missed it again. Both Christian and I looked at each other in disbelief. She really had tuned-out to everything that would prove that there were similarities between her and the South Asian Muslim women she so eagerly looked down upon.

One part of the process was to give the participants an insight to what it meant to fast. We had gone to a 'retreat' in Sheffield, about 10 minutes from my home. We woke the participants up at sunrise, the Fajr prayer, and took them to eat their breakfast. Luke and Hayley were up for the challenge as was Mr Birch, but the others; I have never seen a group of adults prove they could be more childish than children. The Birch children did less moaning and were more willing to participate than their own mother. Her example to her children was, for me, disappointing to say the least. She had partnered with Kerry and Carla as if they had something to prove to us all. I was beginning to wonder why they had taken part. Maybe Kerry thought it would boost her modelling prospects, Carla maybe thought it would be a useful aid for her business and Mrs Birch would have something else to talk to her salon clients about. Either way, I am glad my children were not around to see adults behave in such a way. They had hidden food in their rooms so they could sneak back and nibble during the day. They moaned incessantly about fasting instead of embracing it like Luke, Hayley and Mr Birch. Those three were keen to know why we did it, the deeper meaning to it all, even if they were only asking to be polite, it was more than the others could manage. I truly do believe though that they had a natural curiosity that had to be fulfilled.

I spent a lot of the time watching and listening, using the day to reflect on what I had originally entered this process for. Had I achieved what I had hoped to gain? Was the process making any positive difference to the bridge between Muslim and non-Muslim? It had nothing to do with East and West, I was a Westerner, raised in the West, had heritage that probably dated back to the Vikings, but yet here I was 15 years later believing in what is deemed an Eastern religion when in fact it is a religion for all people, for all of time. When I remember some of the things I heard the other mentors tell the participants, I wondered where they got their information[16]. Some of the things were things I had never heard of or read about, and after 15 years of reading, researching and talking with Muslims from a variety of countries, I came to realise that this is one of the beauties of a religion that spans cultures, countries and language; it fits with everyone. It adds to the beauty of diversity and yet it joins people together who are willing to accept that we are all different, all beautiful in our own way, even if we do not all choose to follow the same path.

There is something profoundly wonderful in accepting others ways and choosing not to follow their ways for yourself. Many of the ideas Mohammad and Suleiman had, I knew I would never choose for my life, just as I explained to Luke, I accept him and my other gay friends wholly and completely, but will never choose the path of homosexuality for myself. I love them all. I accept the different paths that all my friends take, the husbands they choose, the jobs they seek, but their choices are not for me. Of all the participants in the series, I had the greatest amount of respect for Luke. He prayed on time, never missing a prayer. He checked ingredients in food packaging and was upset that the other participants had not taken the process as seriously as they could have done. Hayley was the only other one in the process that I had any respect for. Sitting by the fire all these thoughts overtook me and as the crew came with the dates and the water I felt so emotional at the amount of knowledge on human nature I had gained. I wasn't only thankful for the water and the dates, but also for the distance I had travelled since joining the process. I didn't think the day could get any better. I had a large fire in front of me, and those that know me know I love a big open fire, but when Phil got angry and stormed off to the pub at the end of the road, only to find it had stopped serving food, so he ended up having nothing to eat, the whole group erupted in laughter. God had rewarded him perfectly for his behaviour throughout. Nice one.

The next day we went walking through the Peaks[17]. Rosie, the youngest of the Birch girls, walked with me and we had a great conversation. It was so refreshing and I was impressed that she had so many questions she wanted to ask and ideas she wanted to explore. She was a very impressive young lady, despite many of her mother's bad examples set during the process. She wanted to learn and was genuinely interested. It was a relief to be honest to have someone ask the questions she did, and I hoped that the editing team would include some of the dialogue in the end product, but then again I should have known better. During this walk Phil's language was shocking, and having worked in many kitchens throughout my college days, I had heard a lot of swearing, even done a lot of swearing. I had worked hard since leaving college to improve and clean up my language and it was really hard for me to hear Phil's dirty mouth coming out with swear words every other word, especially as it was coupled with very ignorant, racist views of the world. I asked him to stop swearing, not just because Oscar and Rosie were around us, but also because I didn't like the depth of his swearing. At this point he just let rip and told me to 'stay the fuck away' from him. Gladly Phil, gladly.

I had realised that the visits to Bradford and Dewsbury had gone a long way to just re-enforcing the false myth and perception in the UK that Islaam belonged only to the South Asians, so I had given up on the show in that regard. I had discussed, with my friend Kate, the possibility of pulling out. But we both agreed that so long as I was helping to change the perception of just one person, that would be a job well done.

So far, I felt that we had changed the minds of four in the process, the others I felt were lost causes.

This was proven on one of the last days in the makeshift mosque when the Birch's oldest daughter chose to wear a low-cut top and lie on the floor practically baring her breasts to the men in front of her. She thought she was being clever but all I saw was a disrespectful person wanting to rebel at every opportunity. I got the rebellion thing, being a rebel myself in many ways, but had I even thought about behaving like this, my mum and step- dad would have told me to have more respect for myself, and them. They would have reminded me that I am a reflection of them and the lessons they had taught me. My parents may not be highly educated, well-travelled people, they may have some racist views, but they would never have allowed me to disrespect them, others, or myself in that way. When I shared this tale with my mum, the first thing she asked me was, "What did her mother and father do or say?" When I told her they said and did nothing, her, "Hmmm," said it all. Obviously, Kerry's lifestyle had made an impact on the Birch's daughter rather than the virtues of valuing oneself.

I had been troubled so much since the beginning of the process with the viciousness from Carla and Phil for many reasons. I knew that people took an instant disliking to others, but for it to be acted out through insults and unfounded accusations directly to my face was something quite new, and scary. I had been called a traitor to my country[18] before, but I had never before experienced the venom that came with every interaction. I tried to stay away from Phil and Carla as much as possible, because I knew my patience was running thin. Every day I used to return to the hotel to see my baby and be with my friend Kate, and every day I cried at the nastiness I had experienced at the hands of Carla and Phil.

Things took a turn for the worse with Carla when we went swimming. Just before we got to the swimming pool I realised I had leaked breast milk all over the top I was wearing due to delays with filming. This wasn't a good start but thankfully I had a poncho I could just throw over the top. When we arrived in the changing rooms, we were given Turkish outfits to wear that were similar to Burkinis[19].

These were new to me but the thought of being able to swim again after having chosen to cover was a blessing. I know Carla and Hayley would never understand the depths of the importance this part of the process had on me, how could they? They hadn't asked about the practicalities of being a female Muslim in the UK for a start. There were very few sessions for women only and when I had attended, I had left smelling of curry due to the amount of South Asians that went and just stood in the pool. I am a lane swimmer. I like to swim a minimum of a mile, something I had resigned myself to giving up on since covering. This Burkini thing offered me a gateway to swimming again and having fun with my children without sitting on the side watching them all the time.

My choice to cover was my choice, and I was determined it would not affect my boys lives in a negative way. Plus I did not wish to grow fat and lazy like so many other Muslim women I had come across, who used their loose clothing as much to hide away their fat as they did to dress modestly. God gave me this one body and I had to take care of it as best as I could, especially after all the years I had spent taking drugs.

The insults and mocking came thick and fast from Carla's mouth and it was hard for me to remain calm and quiet. Then I lost it, and for those of you who know me, you know I don't hold back. I wanted to slap her and wake her up from her narrow-minded ignorance but I knew nothing would help her and told her as much. Laura, the producer, then did her best to placate us both, as I don't think any of them had expected me to explode like that.

I then went inside the changing room and calmed down with tears of anger and hurt running down my face. How could I have let someone like her bring me down to her level? Why had I let her ignorance get to me?

I wiped my face, walked out into the swimming area and got in the pool. I swam up and down the lane as if my life depended on it. I felt free. The water felt good and with each stroke my anger ebbed away. I knew I was crying with anger but I was also crying with happiness at being in the water. It felt amazing. I planned to search the internet until I found a stylish version of these Burkini-type things. I was going swimming again, and nothing would stop me.

What did make me feel stronger, though, was seeing both Hayley and Carla too embarrassed to continue wearing the Burkini-thing in public and had changed back into their bikinis. Now who was oppressed by the wider community? And who was stronger in the face of peer pressure? In that moment, I realised how much I had broken free of public opinion. I didn't worry as much about what they thought of me, I didn't feel the pressure to fit in, I was stronger than I had ever been! It didn't bother me that possibly millions of people would see this programme, criticise me and make fun of me for wearing the ugly Burkini-thing. I had found a way to be with my boys in the swimming pool. I had found a way that would allow me to use un-segregated pools with facilities for lane swimmers and get my health back. I was free to start reliving my life in the way I had before I had started covering. I felt at peace. I felt good and nothing was going to spoil that feeling… the feeling of being free.

The day after, we went shopping in a supermarket. We had to show the participants which foods they could buy and which products they should avoid. Again, the participants were left confused due to the products we mentors were allowing them to buy or not buy. Some wouldn't allow them to buy deodorant or nail polish remover with alcohol in. I informed them that in Islaam a lot depended on the intention behind your actions. If they intended drinking the nail polish remover or inhaling the deodorant then, not only did they need therapy, they had to know that both of those are forbidden in Islaam.

I wanted to know about the different styles of food they chose to eat regularly. I helped them to choose items that enabled them to continue eating those foods, just with some tweaking of brands here and there. I did the same with their other household items and explained that just because one Muslim took things to the extreme, they had to remember others chose not to, just as with any religion or set of beliefs. The logic was no different in many cases to other lifestyle choices. Some people chose to spend all their money on cigarettes and alcohol whilst others chose to spend that money on private education. Some people spent all their effort working for success but never got time to enjoy life, and for me, there are so many Muslims that spend too much time considering what is forbidden and the work of the devil instead of enjoying the many things that are allowed and thanking God for everything they have been blessed with.

During this supermarket experience, Phil decided to attack once more and this time I had had enough of his illogical thinking – his blatant disregard for someone else's choice of life – unless it was 'white and English'. When I reminded him that I was white and English he just floundered and started insulting me. I chose to walk away and calm down because not only had I asked him to be more respectful, so had Howard. His nastiness got to a point where I just got up and walked away. I didn't want a repeat of the swimming pool and I know that if I had stayed sitting with them, I would have said many things that I would have regretted and probably slapped him around the face.

Of the other mentors, I disagreed with some of the things they did and said, such as removing the Knight piece in a chess set during the 'contraband' visits. This I could not understand in the slightest. Neither could I accept Mohammad dropping litter in the beautiful Peak District. I had to remind him that God gave us this planet to take care of and he, as a Muslim, should know better than to drop litter. Not to mention the fact he was mentoring others in the way of Islaam. For me, I take the standpoint that it is better to concern ourselves with taking care of our planet and our bodies than removing chess pieces and music from people's homes.

ramO and I had both been through a critical illness, and maybe this process was too soon into my own recovery period, but I don't think about what I can't do and only think about what I can contribute. Taking care of my health is very important to me and I dislike not being able to exercise. I only have one body and I have to take care of it, because if I abuse and neglect it, I will be asked about this on the day of judgement.

I also love music and when I think about how God has created our bodies to receive sound through the invisible sound waves from a piece of vinyl or plastic, that stirs our souls and spread deep and meaningful messages, whether we agree with those messages or not, is a beautiful thing. I know that from my many years of raving, feeling my heart beat with excitement, the butterflies in my stomach and my face break into a smile when I hear the sound of the techno beat, I thank God for the blessing of being able to hear, dance and join with people, creating connections that would never have been made had it not been for the love of music. Each different type of music reaching some one on some level and those that speak of hatred and anger are releasing what is within them. This is not something that should be ignored; it should be listened to and understood. If we then notice a society issue that is causing that anger, then we should all work together to solve it, regardless of who we are and what faith we have. This is one of the things I valued about this process. I may not have agreed with most of the things that the other three mentors said, but there were a lot of things I learnt from them. Many of the things Mohammad and Suleiman brought to the process were based on cultural traditions and beliefs that were so alien to me and things I could not bring into my own lifestyle.

Suleiman had refused to be filmed with me walking through Harrogate town centre at one point, but when I understood why, I respected him much more. His way of respecting his wife and me came out of a deep- rooted sense of honour and love for his wife. I felt honoured to have been part of that. Suleiman has a very gentle soul and he left me wondering how many men, English and non-Muslim, had that much love and respect for their wives. Suleiman's wife is very lucky in that sense.

Mohammad had a wonderful sense of humour and sometimes all we could do was laugh. The only thing that disturbed me a little bit about him was his obsession with Jinn[20]. I even joked with him about it, telling him I could understand his obsession if he was an alcoholic and it was the other Gin he was always thinking about. The joke was lost on him though sadly. Ajmal was different. He was more open-minded and had been raised in the UK like me. We both had a commonsense approach to Islaam, life and shared much of the same humour. We disagreed on a few things, but all in all many of our views were pretty similar. This annoyed many of the participants and I remember being called a traitor again by Phil, but again this was down to his lack of knowledge, lack of respect for others, and his total lack of wanting to learn and get along with people who didn't share his narrow-minded view of the world.

I was relieved when the filming was over. I hoped the editing process would be good and the intention for the show would be honoured. It was a time of waiting and hoping for a positive outcome to something I had done.

About a month later, Christian called me and gave me an update. I was left with a deep sadness with his news. They had decided to call the show *Make Me a Muslim,* one of the worst titles I could have possibly imagined. I had to just wait now for the show to appear on TV. Having done some filming for my own business, and having seen my husband produce a documentary about Arabs in the UK, I knew many of the great bits of footage would end up on the cutting room floor[21]. I had spent three weeks with a group of people to dispel false myths and perceptions of Islaam and the final product would prove whether that had been done or not, and when the show hit the screens, I began to realise the editing team didn't do the three week process any justice at all. There was so much repetition during each episode, and they had edited conversations to the point that the actual meaning of the conversations had been removed. For me the end result was a letdown and I had been plastered all over the nation with phrases taken out of context so that they didn't represent me, or my views of Islaam. They had taken snippets of things and twisted them, and left important bits out. I felt betrayed and lied to, deceived even. This programme had not done what it was supposed to have done. I felt that it had just confirmed stereotypes and hadn't done anything to alter the prejudices that existed. I felt ashamed to have been part of it. I kept thinking that there had to be a follow up to this in the future. How had the process affected the participants, had they changed anything about themselves or their views? I would like to have seen an afterthought piece from the mentors about their experience of the show and what they had learnt. I knew a few of us had found it a useful process, and this for me would have added balance.

I also wasn't prepared for the aftermath as well as I should have been. The viewers of the show I knew would all have their own opinions, and they would share them, as I had done in the past, but I wasn't expecting to be the target of attacks from UK Muslims. That sense of freedom I had felt in the pool slowly drained away from me as I started to read some of the reviews. I had got used to Phil and Carla's attacks but the attacks from fellow Muslim 'sisters' were something else. They were so nasty that it shocked me. Some were even as racist as Phil, saying such things like how could I be a proper Muslim when I wasn't born one or because I wasn't brown! This especially angered me because it is these kinds of Muslims that fuel the rage and hatred towards Islaam and Muslims from people like Phil and Carla.

I had just put myself through three weeks of nastiness and tried to help build bridges, and here were people undoing the good work that I felt had been done. I had done something that I thought would help. I'd spent 21 days away from my four-month-old baby, been in pain due to very full breasts and leaked more than I should have done due to delays caused by egos and ignorance. I'd faced insults and nastiness every day from at least one of the participants; seen what I thought was a valuable process manipulated and destroyed for 'essential viewing pleasure' of the red top and Daily Mail type readers, just to have confirmed what they already, incorrectly, thought. I retreated back into myself.

Unaware to myself, I started suffering from a depression so dark, it would take me a few years to overcome. It was time for me to retreat to my chosen family, my chosen sisterhood, and it was time for me to get a grip on what and who was important in my life.

---

1. This invented word comes from supporters of the English Defence League (EDL). The EDL is a racist and anti-Muslim organisation, and most of its supporters are as ignorant as they are racist, and this word "Muslamics" is a small example of that.
2. I say scholar using quotation marks because I am sure that I study Islaam just as much as, if not more than, many of them, and not just from a pro-Islam point of view either.
3. Or as my mother would say, "His trousers have divorced his ankles and married his knees!"
4. Jungle is a type of dance music played at raves, but many Junglists were more interested in looking like a 'bad-ass' than spreading Peace, Love, and Unity. ramO liked referring to them, unironically, as the "stab wound massive"!
5. Like a long white dress worn by men in the Arab world. Other popular colours are grey or brown.
6. The black and white chequered scarf made famous by P.L.O. leader Yasser Arafat.
7. The "Taqiyya" is the little white hat favoured by Muslim men who think wearing it makes them more pious and therefore a better Muslim. Ironically these hats are not dissimilar to the Kippah, the tiny hat Jewish men are fond of wearing. My research has found nothing about either hat's history that isn't purely cultural.
8. Glamour in this sense means she takes her clothes off for a living and poses topless, with tiny knickers revealing more than they are hiding. There is nothing glamorous about it.
9. Lapsed means he was drinking, taking drugs and eating pork, whilst living with Carla – a similar lifestyle to mine at the beginning of my journey albeit the eating of pig which I find repulsive now.
10. Having read many translations of the Qur'aan, this is one of the best and most moderate with great footnotes, explanations of the time each Surah (verse) was revealed, and it included the verses in English, English transliteration and Arabic.

11. Expressing milk means milking yourself like a cow into a bottle ready for your baby to drink – instead of using formula milk.
12. 'Brad' comes from Bradford and the 'istan' comes from Pakistan. This came about as Bradford has many areas which have high numbers of locals of Pakistani descent.
13. What they call the ninja-style piece of cloth that covers the face, usually of a woman nowadays.
14. There are other stories which state that it was only the women of nobility that wore the niqaab, to separate them from the common folk, and distinguish themselves as women of aristocracy. Who knows which story is true, what's obvious is that the niqaab is cultural not religious.
15. It is a common misconception that Muslim women of South Asian descent have this stay- at-home lifestyle forced upon them. This is true in some cases of course, but it is also true for many women regardless of their ethnicity or religion.
16. One example of this is Mohammad telling the men their trousers should not touch the floor, as it will raise the Jinn up inside of them. Seriously!?
17. The Peak District National Parks, an area of true natural beauty.
18. Surely Christian and Jewish Brits are also traitors to their own country if we use Phil's definition of following a foreign religion; after all Christianity and Judaism were both started by a foreign brown Semite, but I guess logic is also a foreign concept to bigots.
19. The Burkini, from Burka and Bikini, is a full-body covering swimsuit, with trousers and a long sleeved tunic with a head covering attached. This Turkish 'version' of it was indeed hideous to look at, but it was modest, and at that moment that was all I cared about.
20. Jinn are evil spirits.
21. Not literally, I know nowadays things are edited digitally.

EPILOGUE: EGYPT

Getting a grip on things was much harder than I had anticipated. It took a lot out of me and took me on a journey of discovery that has left me with a reflective view on things that can sometimes lead to me spending days mulling things over. It had also made me more determined to make a difference to others, the way I had made a very big difference to my life. I had already realised, when my husband nearly died, that life was too short. But coming to terms with my own critical illness and regaining some of my missing memories had just enforced my desire to do my bit to make the world a better place, to make sure my children had the understanding that we do not throw away opportunities or sit back and watch others suffering when we are in a position to help.

I went into therapy to help me deal with the depression I faced after making the Channel 4 show. It also helped me resolve many issues I had buried deep inside of me from my childhood. I learnt to see how many of the feelings and thoughts I carried around with me were stopping me without me even knowing they were there. I was able to work through my depression in a way that not only relieved me of years of baggage, but also in a way that inspired and motivated me to fulfil the many things I had wanted to do.

My neighbour, Cathy, who had taken care of Khaalid the night before I was admitted to hospital with Naasir, was later diagnosed with Motor Neurone Disease (MND). She was an inspiration to me. I remember watching her from my bedroom window doing Tai Chi in her back garden. She would often go walking with a large backpack into the Peaks. She was a fellow lover of Lapsang Tea, our bonfire tea as we both called it. Her book collection was very impressive and I would always spend time looking at all of them whilst I was visiting her. Watching her decline due to MND was heartbreaking. Here was a wonderfully kind lady, intelligent, wise, and as fit as a fiddle, being debilitated by an awful disease that had killed her two older sisters, her uncle, and her father[1]. I was determined to help raise awareness and cash for MND, and the building of a new scientific research facility based in Sheffield. It was going to be the leading neurological facility in the world.

I decided I would put on a fashion show to raise money for Sheffield Institute for Translational Neurosciences – SiTRAN[2] – and Motor Neurone Disease (MND). During this process, I realised that there were many more prejudices in my life and one or two people I considered friends showed me they too were blinded by their own prejudices about Muslims. A friend designed an outfit especially for the event that saw me humiliated in many ways, something that put a very large distance between us. The fashion show itself was a success as we raised over 10K for the centre. Looking back, I also realised that I was stronger than I thought, as I had to stand on stage to speak to hundreds of people, including the city's fashionistas, about a serious subject, dressed like a bloody Genie that had escaped from his magic lamp!

I also had the goal of wanting to run a marathon, so having never entered an official 'race' I entered the Sheffield Half Marathon 2009, giving me a year to get fit. I was determined to make it through the finish line either on my feet or on my knees, even if it took me all week to do it. The challenges with this would test me more physically and mentally than giving birth ever did.

I had always wanted to go and live in the Arab world and walk the lands of the Prophets. I knew that I had set myself a deadline of leaving the UK by the time my eldest son was six, giving us three to four years to learn Arabic before returning to the UK for the boys to complete their secondary education before choosing any university in the world that they wanted, if they wanted to go to university, that is.

Moving to any other country was going to be hard, as I had never lived outside of England. It would be especially hard going to a country with a very different climate, a different language with a different character set and direction of reading. I was going to be away from my girls, the chosen family, and reform my relationship with ramO who had been away working overseas for much of the last seven years. How homesick would I get? How would the boys adjust? How would their education be affected? So many things I had believed about myself would change, as would my view of Islaam and the Egyptian populous. My view of life would change beyond measure and what would make the move an even bigger transformation was the day I had planned to take my eldest son to the Cairo Museum, in the heart of Tahrir Square, would turn out to be the day the Egyptian Revolution would start.

With one phone call I knew our lives would never be the same again. Living through the Uprising, the first democratic elections Egypt has ever seen and the changing view of foreigners would provide both ramO and I opportunities that would never happen in the UK, as well as put a massive strain on us as a family. Would it bring us closer together or tear us all apart?

---

1. Even wheelchair bound she was still more active, and more of an activist, than most Muslim British women, going on peace marches regularly with the Stop The War and Palestinian Solidarity Campaign organisations.
2. http://sitran.dept.shef.ac.uk/

GRATITUDE

Thank you to all those who helped me to write this book, especially ramO, who edited the book. You were my husband for 18 years, and I would not have been able to achieve many of the things I have without your support and encouragement.

To Khaalid, my prince, and Naasir, my soldier, thank you for being you, for your hugs, your kisses and for keeping me going every single day. You have taught me so much about myself and I pray God rewards you both abundantly in all areas of life always. You are amazing, and what you think, feel and wish to say is important. God gave you a voice, so use it, always, remember that.

A HUGE thank you to Joe Dobson for coming up with the name of my book. It was so obvious I missed it completely!

For the cover design I have to thank the design genius, Jerry Lampson. For leaving me speechless, which doesn't happen very often, I have to thank my dear friend Charles Lovibond for the wonderful job he did on the foreword.

Huge thanks go to my dear friend, Dr Alison Buxton, who has been with me every step of the way.

And to Laura Collinson, Mark Smith, Lix Yoxall, Sigrun Valsdottir, Rowaida Shahwan and Omar Kandeel who gave their valuable feedback. What you will read is a result of their feedback. I did listen to some of it, I promise!

Thank you to my mum who taught me to always do my best and to know 'there is no such word as can't'. Hearing you say these words in my head has given me the drive to always do my best and believe I can do anything.

Without the support of my friends Amira Adams, Rosie Khan, Debbie Miller I would never have had the spa sessions and endless cake and coffees to keep the original drafts going.

To my dearest friend, Jamie Stevenson, for just being you.

And to my chosen brothers, Rob Staff and Alan Richardson, for standing by me through all the phases of my life.

Thank you also goes to Ahmed el Fiky, Suzanna Egan-Mitchell, Sarah Thabit and Yasmine ElAbd for their continuous support and encouragement in the final stages of this book coming together.

And finally, so much love and thanks to Linda Diggle, who has supported me through the ups and downs of writing *Walaahi* and *Crossing The Line*, my second and third books, and helping me understand where I want to be taking my career as an author, and author coach. Your support, encouragement and knowledge have been so valuable, and I feel so blessed to have you in my life, and on this journey with me.

ABOUT THE AUTHOR

Dawn Bates is a serial entrepreneur, business mentor, global thought leader and author coach.

Dawn's writing is honest, frank and engaging, bringing humour and powerful insights to all who read her work.

She is also the author of a plethora of articles for various global publications covering a multitude of subjects.

A powerful instigator of change, Dawn creates exceptional results by making people rethink their life, whilst discovering and harnessing the greatest freedom of all: their own truth. She's an authority on leading others, igniting passions and purpose within the individual self, shifting them from fear, feelings of imposter and self-doubt to living an inspired and joyful life on their own terms.

Please take a selfie of yourself with the book
and share it with me on social media.

facebook.com/RealDawnBates

instagram.com/realdawnbates

twitter.com/realdawnbates

linkedin.com/in/dawnbates

And if you would also write a review that would be great!

Thank you!

Lightning Source UK Ltd.
Milton Keynes UK
UKHW010033230422
401922UK00003B/719